RT
The Reverse Theory

ARE YOU READY TO
EXPAND YOUR MIND

PREPARE TO BE AMAZED

Published in 2010 by Christopher Ball

THE PRIORY
BRIGHTON
BN3 3RT

CONDITION OF SALE

All Rights Reserved

A catalogue record of this book is available from the British Library

ISBN – 978 0 9564761
Edited by Inspired Expression
Designed & Printed in Great Britain by Concept Print

www.reversetheory.com

The Tale of the Humble Beach Pebble

Please send any constructive contributions for the next
edition of RT to info@reversetheory.com

New light has been thrown
on the origins of mankind

Discover how the humble beach pebble
reveals how the pyramids were built thus
uncovering an equation to another dimension.

This book will change the course of history

This book will change you

Life on this planet will never be the same again

Prepare to be amazed

This book is the beginning of a new era of thought. Each and every one of us will feel the astounding effects of RT. Poised to change the world's thinking, you will learn why the humble beach pebble reveals how the pyramids were built; you will discover the soul wrenching story of Hell and the true meaning of sacrifice and, ultimately, this exceptional book will present you with the tools to ascertain the true age of this planet and the truth behind the real human evolution... *Move over Mr Darwin, you've got competition!*

Reverse Theory will open your mind and change the way you think; it will give you a glimpse into the unknown and offer you freedom to your afterlife. If you are ready to open your mind, then wisdom is heading your way.

If you are ready for a new tomorrow RT will lead you there.

A NOTE TO THE READER

I was forty years old before I knew the difference between writing 'there and their, where and were, wear and ware etc. And as I cannot spell, read or write particularly well, writing this book has been a feat within itself!

Academically I left school with enough skill to sign my name, (hooray for Microsoft Word) So, when it came down to putting my thoughts in writing, I had to enlist help from a very good friend of mine, Sara. She took my words and rewrote them into something readable. Between us we edited and rewrote the Reverse Theory until the final draft was settled upon. I'm thankful that Sara managed to curb if not all, certainly most, of my 'Chris'isms'.

That hurdle and decision aside, what I did possess were the skills of politeness, patience and thought, (thank you Mum and Dad). I was born with an enquiring mind, an innate confidence in myself and my discoveries and the confidence that would allow me to fly smack-bang in the face of reason.

I also have my comforting and, to me, naturally occurring beliefs and knowledge that this world, this universe, which we are travellers within, is so vast, so miraculous, so mis-understood and so much more intricate than any of us can possibly imagine; and even more so after reading this book.

These gifts have meant that for me, flying in the face of reason is no hardship, simply part of what must be done. It is my path, my destiny, to share my truths so that others may benefit from the knowledge and affect their own lives accordingly.

Amen to that.

CONTENTS

INTRODUCTION

My name is Christopher Way Ball and I am writing this book from my heart and my head. I cannot profess to be a writer, and despite giving it my best shot, I had to enlist help to get my words, thoughts and feelings down on paper.

Many of the following words, as I indicated previously, were therefore written with Sara's invaluable help. Without her there would be no revelations, or book, just blocks of information and random thoughts held within an old tatty manuscript collecting dust, with little structure or meaning despite the enlightening and energising content. I do, however, feel happy and excited, even elated, that the original text held and the new text still holds more truth than I ever originally realised. That whilst I've had help to put my thoughts and words in some understandable order, the revelations I have had and the truths that have been given to me, are some of the most intriguing and exciting discoveries that this universe has to offer.

I hope you will keep an open mind as you read my book. I hope, also, that you will allow yourself to consider that all new truths may be difficult, yet not impossible, to accept; that a multitude of scholars, scientists, historians, gurus, and discoverers over the ages, have been met with disbelief and disdain, as they put their reputations on the line and presented the world with new ideas built on new facts. After all, once upon a time it was thought this world was flat. It's worth noting that these same people of science are now held in extremely high regard.

So with this in mind, as you read, consider these points and put your current thinking to one side as you embrace new possibilities: possibilities which I believe to be categorically true.

WHY SELF-PUBLISHING?

Firstly, I would like to comment on why I have self-published this book.

Over the past twenty years I have tried to catch the interest of many different publishers and publishing agents all over the world, but to no avail. I have contacted the top scholars from a number of universities, including Oxford and Cambridge. I have written to science magazines and newspapers from around the globe, again, all to no avail. I have also broadcast a brief outline of these revelations on national radio, but my words fell on deaf ears and I was mildly ridiculed. Presumably the daunting task of changing current beliefs was too uncomfortable for them.

Perhaps the idea of rewriting science literature was far too complicated for 'experts' to contemplate. Perhaps many people from all walks of life are unwilling, even scared, to contemplate new possibilities in areas which have been indoctrinated into the world as categorical truths. I've realised from painful trial and error that the majority of people tend to be stuck in their views; and, particularly, only accepting of new theories when they are delivered by reputable fellow scientists. A scientist I am not, but a seeker of the truth I most certainly am.

For the most part, when dealing with scholars of science, I have been treated like a crackpot with a crackpot theory. My ideas have been met with disregard even before I opened my mouth to reveal my thinking. It's amazing how closed minded people are before they've even listened; listened to something which touches so many areas of their lives. It's far more comfortable for them to hold on to their current thinking and not budge from it; to not allow previously unknown others to provide some new awareness to their thinking. This is comfort in the familiar, I guess. 'I know what I like and I like what I know': a phrase usually associated with certain Brits in a foreign clime, sampling (or rather not sampling) new cuisines, but a phrase that is quite apt here. After all, I have been asking people to sample something new; to take on something previously unheard of; un-thought of.

In the defence of the scholars, however, I guess the discoveries I'm about to reveal are so farfetched that they really are quite unbelievable and perhaps more so if you have a PhD in science and believe your science books are your gospel. After all: when you study, for years, books that you consider to be the truth, books that came to you as firm truths in the first place, in order to change your thinking and beliefs you would have to assume that the books were wrong. And surely we couldn't have that could we?

Well, I believe we could.

My discoveries go completely against the grain of accepted scientific thinking and against so much that we have been told, taught and seen, nevertheless I believe them to be true.

So convinced am I that I have chosen to self-publish this book. But, you know, when you believe in something this strongly, and you want to share it with the world for the good of mankind, there really is no other choice; no matter how hard the task.

A FEW MYSTERIES OF OUR WORLD

There are many unanswered questions in this world of ours. Many mysteries that have been with us for centuries: The missing link, how mankind came to be on this planet, evolution, God, how the pyramids were built, the demise of the dinosaurs, Stonehenge, the human spirit, whether life is a product of chance or intelligent design, Heaven, the afterlife...the list is endless and is an ever growing fascination with those whose minds have any part of the seeker gene.

There are many theories, many books, written on many subjects; differing religions; each claiming to have the ultimate answer, and differing sciences; each informing the world that they are right. Within the scientific world, there are many subjects each with their own truths but they don't always agree with each other.

I have spent many years considering the different viewpoints of various scholars who argue amongst themselves as to the truth of an issue. So, I would say it's fair to say that for many of life's mysteries the jury is still out and, regarding all the theories, no matter how convinced the theorists may be of their own truths, nothing is set in stone.

Or is it?

Ha, I have to laugh at the last phrase because, as far as I'm concerned, many answers certainly are, indeed, set in stone.

Regardless, we all enjoy a good mystery and I'm sure we've all wondered about things like evolution, God, how the pyramids were built, to name but a few. I'm certain that each and every one of us has questioned our own thoughts and viewpoints. We may have dwelled for a long time, we may have fleetingly touched upon the subjects before moving on to something else but I'd say that the truth of the matter is: we are all intrigued.

Perhaps we trust that one day, in one way or another all these universal mysteries will be answered. I believe that day has arrived.

Welcome to a new tomorrow.

I sincerely believe that this book solves many of the unanswered or, at least, wrongly answered truths such as: the age of this planet, how the pyramids were built and whether or not we evolved from primates.

I believe these mysteries and questions are unsolved and

unanswered because something is wrong, something is wrong with our understanding of life; something is missing from our facts and figures. Now though, the missing piece of the jigsaw has been found. No longer will we fumble around in the dark. No longer will we be lost within an entanglement of unknown mysteries.

I have discovered a missing link, not Darwin's missing link but the missing link of information between what is thought to be true and what is actually true; and I must add: the truth may seem stranger than fiction.

Science is built on facts, and by using as many facts as possible geologists, mathematicians, scientists and physicists, through observation and experiment, have pieced together a puzzle of knowledge in an attempt to understand how the physical world works. In their attempts to understand how the physical world works they have pieced together fragments of information to discover the truth about our existence. To discover the truth about our existence they have used a widely accepted 'fact' from the natural and physical world. However, to grasp this systematic study and to encompass the structure of the physical and the natural world they have unmistakably and fundamentally dropped the biggest clanger of all time.

As a result, our understanding of natural science has held a defect since the beginning of recorded time. This information has been collated and analysed using past discoveries and current methodologies, but also a certain amount of speculation and educated guesswork. Guesswork which I believe has caused our facts and figures to be wrongly diagnosed and miscalculated. This in turn has led to a stream of other inaccuracies. So, what happens if science has miscalculated? It's certainly not far from the realms of possibility. After all, science is evolving and building all the time. Facts that were once assumed as true have been disputed and replaced as new facts have come to light. Discoveries are made and, in turn, previous discoveries and formed understandings have doubt shed upon them. Ideas are presented and viewpoints are changed.

Change is the natural order of life and so we should all be open to it and embrace it, after all we cannot avoid it. In fact: change is the one constant and, bearing this is mind, I ask you to open up your mind to a new era of thought; a new viewpoint altogether. By all means keep hold of what you had but perhaps put it to one side for a moment while you give some thought to these new theories and revelations.

These revelations were given to me in a very spiritual way and in a way which I could not ignore, no matter how hard I tried; hence I present you with this book. As shocked and confused as I was with the initial information, the more I thought about it and the more I focused on its possibilities, the more it was impossible to avoid and the more truths I began to see. Once I accepted these truths, my mind went on to receive other understandings which related, as if by magic, to the first truth and I realised how intrinsically linked these new revelations were and what an impact they had on life as we know it.

This book will look at correcting one small geological misobservation and, by doing so, answer many unanswered questions and solve many unsolved mysteries. By adjusting one small geological misunderstanding, earth science will be turned upside down and inside out, forever, to such an extent that it will be necessary to rewrite the science books. In other words ... start all over again!

HOW OLD IS OUR PLANET?

This is an important place to start but no less important than any of the other sections. I would simply like to pose this question first as I believe we have over-estimated the answer. The entirety of what that means exactly, only time will tell.

There are many theories offered on the age of this planet and many differing points of view. The intrinsic arguments seem to be between science, with its physics and radiometric dating techniques, and religion, with its faith and biblical scriptures. Scientists believe they have proved that Planet Earth is several billion years old and I'll explain how in a moment; whereas Young Earthers, siding with religion, estimate that we are residing on a planet which is no more than a few thousand years old.

They believe that the earth cannot be old, for various reasons. The Bible is the first and foremost point of reference, and using the times, dates and ages of people in the Bible, the figure of six thousand or so years is reached.

There are also scientific reasons why young earthers believe that this planet is thousands rather than billions of years old. These are:

Galaxies wind themselves up too fast

There are too few super remnants

Comets disintegrate too quickly

There is not enough mud on the sea floor

There is not enough sodium in the sea

The earth's magnetic field is decaying too fast

Many strata are too tightly bent

Fossil radioactivity shortens geologic 'ages' to a few years

There is too much helium in minerals

There is too much carbon 14 in deep geologic strata

There are not enough Stone Age skeletons

Agriculture is too recent

History is too short.

At this point I have purely listed these reasons, in brief, as I do not wish to detract from RT's main theme. I do however go on to explain them more fully towards the end of the book, for those who are interested.

Scientists have studied the physical forces of the planet

and come up with their answers: after taking into account geological dating of rocks and fossils, science (based on radiometric dating) dates this planet at around 4.6 billion years old.

From a scientific point of view, in order to work out the age of planet earth, it is vital to know how old the rocks upon it are. Unlike carbon dating which is only accurate up to fourteen thousand years, radiometric dating (radioactive dating) has an accuracy of many billions of years based on mathematical physics. Each and every rock (some more than others) contains chemical elements that decay from one element to another. These are unstable atoms known as isotopes, where the ratio of the parent isotope gives way to the daughter elements. Products like radioactive uranium give off invisible rays of energy which gradually change the uranium into lead and likewise with potassium to argon, and rubidium to strontium. Scientists, through their testing, have discovered how long it takes for the element of uranium to change into lead, so by comparing how much uranium and how much lead are in the atom and likewise the rock, they believe they can determine the age of the planet.

Using this method, scientists have determined that some granite rocks found in Africa, Canada, Australia and many other countries, are around 3.5 billion years old. Parts of meteors which have fallen to earth are apparently even older. They are, allegedly, parts of other planets from our universe and nearly every fallen meteorite has the same composition as the earth with an age bordering on 4.6 billion years old.

To back this up: many scientists believe that the complete Cosmos started at the same time, around 9 billion years ago: The Big Bang Theory. This leads them to the same estimation of the earth forming approximately 4.6 billion years ago.

Now, I do not intend this book to start out as a debate between science and religion. Clearly each side of the argument has its own very staunch reasons and viewpoints for being absolutely correct. These are age old discussions. What I do intend to do, however, is offer an alternative viewpoint which may support both sides in some ways. I certainly believe that Planet Earth is nowhere near as old as current scientific viewpoints would have us believe, but the important point here is that I'm going to unveil a discovery which will show that calculations have been based upon incomplete studies and that the age of this planet has been incorrectly calculated. After that, it is up to the scientists and geologists, the Young Earthers and Deep Timers, to use that information to ascertain an exact age.

The fact that I believe that earth is young may seem like I am siding with faith and religion. Don't get me wrong, I am a great believer that life is an intelligently designed creation however I'm not siding with or going against any current religion, merely offering an alternative solution. Likewise, I am not siding with or going against science. Science has given us incredible insights and will continue to do so. No, instead, I am offering information that will go on to reveal the truth and whether that helps either 'side' or indeed both 'sides' is a matter for time to reveal.

Maybe RT will go on to partially prove one or the other side, or even both. Maybe these new findings will go on to uncover some additional facts which either side, or indeed both sides, hadn't considered. We don't know yet. This is the beginning of some new truths, and these new findings are at the beginning of a new trail which will help lead us to working out the age of this planet effectively, and solve a few mysteries in the process. I would like to add that once my theory is looked into, I will expect geologists and creationists alike to put it to the test, thus proving or disproving their own theories.

To be honest, I believe that the mathematics (the sums behind the dating of the planet) is wrong. I also believe that science will eventually prove my words, prove my theories, and that one day this will be looked upon as a book which changed the world and the course of history.

THE FLAW WITHIN GEOLOGY

Since time began mankind has been searching for answers to their existence. Since time began we have wondered about and pursued answers to life's greatest mysteries. We have asked about what happened in our history and tried to find definite answers as to whether we have been created or have come about as a by product of evolution. We have been told that we have come from apes and this planet is billions of years old, yet still there are sceptics. But there is so much evidence; why should we dispute it?

I'll tell you why: because the very first page or the very first stake in the ground that led us to believe this planet was old, was wrong. Wrong to such a degree that our imagination has snowballed out of all proportion and distorted all that followed. So many theories, hypotheses and figures that made up our understanding of this planet, even our understanding of time itself have been distorted. So much of what we know about this planet based on time, particularly deep-time (time measurement used by science to ascertain and compare events over the course of Earth's history), is incorrect. I sometimes wonder whether the speed of light has also been miscalculated.

A simple geological stake in the ground first put a time span to geology. This in turn gave us our perception of deep-time. This perception of deep-time then went on to lay the foundations to mathematical physics.

This simple concept dated the rock strata and the geological column (the fossilized subdivision of geological time) within the rock strata. All three had a hand in constructing the theory of evolution, and all four theories combined laid the foundations for calculating the physics behind radiometric dating.

By applying this mathematical conundrum through the principle of radioactive isotopes, the planets age was calculated as being 4.6 billion years old. All these facts and figures backed each other up and contributed to a fundamental error brought about by this simple stake in the ground.

Over the years, the centuries and millenniums, we have been seeing a true fact of life ... not a theory, not a hypothesis, a real fact of life quite literally in reverse. We've been looking at a natural occurrence the wrong way round. An optical illusion has befallen mankind on an unprecedented scale and sent our thoughts and understandings tumbling in the wrong direction.

As a result, geological science has written, quite adamantly and rigid in their views, that this planet is old when in fact, based on these new findings, the planet and the geological column are comparatively young. This one misunderstanding, based on such a small part of geology, has been continuously added to and built upon, thus distorting our thinking, our books, theories and hypotheses. It's amazing how something as small as a grain of sand, could have such catastrophic implications, but in this case it does. You could compare this misunderstanding to launching a rocket and sending it on a course to the moon, but accidentally putting in the wrong coordinates. One degree out, and you would miss the target by miles.

The main part of this amazing discovery is so simple, that once you allow yourself to accept it, you will probably laugh at its simplicity. But as this revelation lies in uncharted territory you will have to make up your own mind as to its authenticity.

If you can accept what I'm about to reveal, other revelations will fall into place: like understanding how the pyramids were built, which is so obvious and so simple that it proves my first point. You'll see that there really can't be any other way!

Both discoveries uncover answers to a multitude of other unanswered questions and in turn many unsolved mysteries and enigmas fall into place. You can smile with confidence as you peep through into the unknown and if you are spiritually inclined you are in for a real treat, because at long last the pyramids have revealed their secret. Life is a continuum. When you die, you simply continue, you and your thoughts grow and expand in a different dimension. You can never stop thinking.

You may have reasons for not being able to accept what I am about to unveil: perhaps you are unable to think outside the box. You may have been brainwashed with a PhD in science; I say brainwashed as, if something is said, taught, often enough there is a tendency to believe it is true. Perhaps my revelation will go so far against the grain of your chosen philosophy that you cannot, or will not, accept it. Whatever the reason, I still implore you to keep an open mind as, if you don't, you may never completely understand life. You may never understand the mysteries that life holds. Those mysteries will never be answered as your train of thought will be going in the wrong direction; as it has been doing since the birth of Homo sapiens. Thousands of years of speculation upon speculation, guess work upon guess work. Years upon years of misguided thinking; *ouch!*

The clues are there for all to see; science and your immediate common-sense, however, will swear that I am wrong; but it is up to you look at these new facts, take in all the new clues, take your time and make up your own mind. ***Do not dismiss this discovery without thought***. Look at the bigger picture and think outside the box and you will see the true meaning of life and, indeed, beyond the subconscious.

There is an old saying: 'Believe half of what you see and nothing of what you hear' and our indoctrinated beliefs and our understanding of life are no exception to the instruction of this wise guidance.

Our very first observation which processed our perception of time was camouflaged, hidden; hidden within another process; hidden within another fact of life which makes it impossible to see. It is not that it is invisible to the naked eye, far from it, it is very noticeable once pointed out, and very understandable when considered. Sometimes we cannot see the woods for the trees and this is a fine example.

A pebbled beach, the humble beach pebble; ever thought about where they came from?

Coastal erosion is a fact of life, a fact of life happening everyday and happening before our very eyes but it is coastal erosion that has camouflaged this revelation.

Commonsense tells us that sand is a process of erosion: solid rock erodes to form boulders, boulders erode to form pebbles, and pebbles erode to form sand. Commonsense tells us that all the sand in the world has come about by the process of erosion, and that's a lot of sand. A process clearly seen and clearly understood, a natural process taking (according to the encyclopaedias of science) aeons: an aeon being an indefinite amount of time equal to approximately a thousand million years. In other words: a major division of geological time. To give you examples: the first aeon in the Earth's history is called the Hadean, followed by the Archaean period: thought to be some four billion years ago.

It may seem logical that this planet is old. It must be old. I mean look at all the sand in the world that has come about as a result of the erosion from solid rock. Think of how long, how many centuries, how many aeons that process must have taken. There really is no other explanation; so it seems...

Geologists, mathematicians and scientists have clearly studied erosion and pondered upon how long it has taken nature to produce all the sand in the world. There would have been studies and discussions and theories and new theories and finally a decision will have been reached; a decision which the encyclopaedias will have been given to take to print.

I quote from an encyclopaedia:

SAND: solid rock is broken down by wind, rain, and frost, leaving the more resistant rocks in large fragments. These large fragments then roll around grinding against each other along the seashores, where, through the ages, they lose their rough edges and become gravel and sand.

AGE – A vast division of geological time.

When calculating the age of Planet Earth, our first learned scholars reached the answer 'aeons'. I repeat, an aeon is a rough estimate of one thousand million years. So, the scientific deity and pillars of society have made it known by voicing and recording their opinion as: 'This planet is old'.

This means that geological time is old, the geological column is old, the planet is old, the rocks are old, creation is old and, perhaps most importantly, the theory of evolution is the most likely explanation for mankind's existence.

However, and with the utmost respect to the great scholars of the world, this theory is wrong; *very* wrong.

THE REVERSE THEORY – EXPLAINED
THE MYSTERY OF OUR SHORELINES

I'd like you to think about a beach; a pebbled beach. This is where the Reverse Theory will start. I am going to explain where those pebbles have come from and how reversed our thinking needs to be in order to understand the errors in the geological stake in the ground.

As I have explained, geologists, mathematicians and scientists first dated the age of this planet on their understanding of rocks, and then used their radioactive dating methods to find an exact age, but what happens if the overall mechanics for dating those rocks was incorrect in the first instance, before radioactive dating was even invented? How would that affect the overall mathematical picture? And what would that mean when looking into our planets past, our planets future and hence into mankind's future?

Well, we'll know soon enough because I'm about to reveal my secret: the secret of the pebbles: the Reverse Theory. Here goes, are you ready? Be prepared!

You know how we assume that solid rock becomes boulders and boulders become pebbles and pebbles become sand? Well, you know what? That is completely wrong! It's quite the reverse! Our pebbled beaches were not formed by erosion.

Quite simply, where seashores are lapped by dirty polluted seawater, beach pebbles are formed by the principle of 'tidemark' and, most certainly, not from the principle of erosion.

Pebbles are formed by deposits of pollution and lime-filled polluted seawater that hardens when exposed to the elements. They are created by a microscopic drawn out process of layer building: a layer-upon-layer, wet and dry growth process. Pebbles get bigger not smaller. Beach pebbles and sand are NOT formed by aeons of solid rock erosion, pebbles are formed by tidal accretion; they are formed by the principle of an increasing succession of tidemarks.

As bizarre as this may or may not seem, I simply ask you to consider it. Just have a think and you will never view seashores in the same way again. This is where putting your previous misconceptions to one side comes in.

Pebbles, good old fashioned beach pebbles, which some of us have been used to seeing all our lives, get bigger not smaller. Now then, what does this mean? Well, if you consider that it has been assumed that pebbles grinding down to sand has taken aeons: ages and ages, then, this is wrong! One of the most obvious premises for calculating deep time and the age of this planet is so completely incorrect that everything relating to the principle of geology is clearly flawed; even commonsense comes under scrutiny.

Think of this in real terms. Think of the process. Take a look on your local pebbly beach if you like. Pick up some sample pebbles and take a look at how they are formed. Some have clearly defined layers all the way round them; layers that have built up over the years.

Twice a day our shores are lapped by incoming tides, twice a day pollutants are deposited onto the shore, and twice a day the warmth of the land and the effect of the elements dry this tidemark, a giant tidemark. Roughly every twelve and a half hours our seashores are lapped by incoming tides. Each time the tide retreats it leaves behind a microscopic fingerprint of pollution, sea debris and lime deposit (calcium carbonate: calcite from marine organisms) which is dried by the atmosphere. Remember: it's important to note at this point, that lime may start soft but it becomes incredibly hard and is the main element for concrete; I will come to this, in more detail, later in the book. As the days, months and years go by each layer dries to form an additional layer of hardened sediment. And, remember: the sea is filled with all kinds of pollutants: the sea's, pollution, pollutants from the atmosphere and human pollution. Everything adds to the building process.

From sand, over the years, pebbles grow. Clusters of sand will stick together and form divots within the clusters. Then the next incoming tide fills these divots and the process continues until grit is formed. Each layer of accretion will continue to build up until the perfect pebbles are formed. As the tide pushes the pebbles up the beach, the larger pebbles are heavy enough to stay there, thus leaving them high up the beach away from the bashing of the waves.

Sand, however, cannot dry underwater so, from the tidemark outwards, it will always remain sandy. But from there inwards and up the beach, thin layers of deposited silt slowly build up, each layer part-solidifying before the next incoming tide arrives, very slowly cementing many grains of sand together, like sandstone. These compounded grains are slowly pushed up the beach by the incoming tides where the process is repeated over and over again until large grit is formed.

As each layer begins to receive the full benefit of the sun and the wind's drying time, the scum and grime and lime scale in the water slowly cements many grains of sand together (I use the word cement quite appropriately here as cement, in today's building processes, is formed primarily from lime, which makes it incredibly hard) These forming pebbles are slowly pushed up the beach, over the years, by the incoming tides, where of course they are exposed to that little more drying time. There, the same thing happens, layer upon layer of grime and sea debris, added to that little more

A selection of pebbles found at my local beach

Tidal surf on pebbled beach – Whitstable, Kent (photo courtesy of Joe Django)

No tidal current, hence no pebbles

The cleaner the tidal water the smaller the pebbles

Waves breaking on pebbled beach – Whitstable, Kent, (photo courtesy of Joe Django)

Chalk cliffs such as the White Cliffs of Dover have a white tidemark which result in white pebbles

A white pebble beach under chalk cliffs

The build up of lime scale in a kettle and lime scale from leaking pipes

drying time, cements and bonds these larger pieces together until odd-shape larger grit is formed. This process continues until the grit becomes gravel, gravel becomes shingle, shingle becomes small pebbles, and small pebbles become larger pebbles. It's the complete reverse to the currently accepted process.

When these pebbles are forming, of course there is a process of bashing together which wears the edges more smoothly; hence we see the pebbles in their current state.

When these still-forming pebbles become too big and heavy, the outgoing tides have difficulty drawing them back down again. The incoming tides do, however, have the strength to slowly push these pebbles high up the beach leaving them in great mounds at the top.

Now, here's an important point: If you were to assume that pebbles grind down to sand, then surely sand should be found within the rougher shorelines where rougher waves would have been responsible for grinding and bashing the pebbles together to make this abundance of sand; and pebbles, boulders and the more solid rock should be within the calmer shores as they wouldn't have the forceful waves to bash and erode them. We would simply have calm seas with an abundance of cliffs and rocks. It would make sense, wouldn't it? But this is not the case. Sunny climates have sand whilst rougher climates have pebbles.

Here's another very important point to note: Pebbles are a smooth rounded shape, whereas sand is square, angular and jagged. Pebbles grinding down as the textbooks suggest is, therefore, implausible.

And something else to think about, here: Pebbles generally have a light multi-coloured exterior with a very black interior, whereas sand is mainly yellow in colour, meaning if pebbles were reducing in size sand would be dark in colour.

Take the white cliffs of Dover, the Seven Sisters, or the white cliffs along certain areas in Sussex, England. The cliffs are white as they are made of chalk (with the odd layer of flint) Many of the pebbles that lay at their base are white, sometimes pearl white. It would be impossible to create solid pebbles from chalk, they would simply disintegrate. However, seeing as many pebbles are white, it begs the question why and where did they come from. Quite simply, the chalk is washed from the cliff face into the sea, by the elements and then the same process happens as it would on any other pebbled beach; the white chalk forms part of the debris and lime which coats the sand to create the pebbles, hence they turn out white.

The makeup of pebbles, the colour, is dependent on geological whereabouts, for instance: pebbles at the base of a white cliff are basically white whereas pebbles at a more commercial area would be brown to reflect the water colour.

CHALK CLIFFS

Think about why you have bigger pebbles on the surface layer of beaches and smaller ones underneath. It's because the sun is less often able to dry the lower layers and therefore the pebbles on those layers take longer to form. Growing pebbles! Who'd have thought it? Crazy, eh? Yes ... but think about it; it's true!

Think of a teaspoon or teacup which tarnishes from tea. Think of a basin, bath or sink which is never cleaned and the tidemark that the dirty water leaves behind.

Let's look at this example in more detail. Consider what happens after you've used a basin. A thin layer of scum, grime and lime scale builds up above the water line and when the water is drained, you are left with a tidemark. The longer you leave this tidemark the harder it becomes to clean off. Think of how hard it would become if you never cleaned it. OK, some of this tidemark is dead skin particles and dirt and will gradually wash away, and certainly be easy enough to clean, but the lime scale which is inherent in our waters is an important element here. This, if you were to leave it on your basin, would, over time, grow hard and very difficult to shift.

Let's take another example: think of the amount of lime scale that builds up within hard water areas. Take, for instance, the south coast of England where I come from. It borders the channel and is considered a very hard water area. Our water is notorious for coating our pipes and shower heads. Here we see a photo of some particularly badly affected pipes.

Think of the kettles and how, if you don't de-scale them, they become encrusted with blocks of hardened white lime scale. As you can see in this photo, this can build up into great mounds within your kettle, believe me I've tried it.

The build up of lime scale in a kettle and lime scale from leaking pipes

Another rather lovely example of a very similar growth process is a pearl. Consider a pearl within an oyster shell. It didn't start out like that, it grew. The pearl grew by accretion, and here's the clever bit, it grew from a grain of sand! Natural pearls are nearly 100% calcium carbonate and conchiolin. It is thought that natural pearls form under a set of accidental conditions when a microscopic intruder or parasite enters a bivalve mollusc, and settles inside the shell. The mollusc, being irritated by the intruder, secretes the calcium carbonate and conchiolin to cover the irritant. This secretion process is repeated many times, thus producing a pearl. Natural pearls come in many shapes and sizes, with perfectly round ones being comparatively rare. Sound familiar? This is just like pebbles. It's a different method of accretion, but the process is very similar. Perhaps we could learn a lot from this. I mean, think about it, in many ways, the world really is our oyster! Everything, physical and unseen, that comes from each and every one of us has an impact on our surroundings which grow and change accordingly.

You should have the picture now, so simply transfer this process onto a shoreline and we have the makings of a pebbled beach. It's the exact same principle but in the case of a shoreline we have a combination of conglomerates and fusion and all sorts of pollutants hitting our shores

SOME OTHER INTERESTING POINTS TO BACK RT
Micro fossils and part of the story they tell

Let's now think about the fossils that continue to be discovered in our pebbles. You can see that at some stage these creatures have been embedded inside them. The pebble formation process has literally happened around them. These dead creatures were encased, slowly but surely, within the build up process, being coated and immortalised in drying layers of slowly hardening water debris.

Sure, it is a fact, that some fossils are found in larger rocks, rocks which have had layers of earth, mud and limestone laid on top of them, thus burying them there; and perhaps some would say that those larger rocks have been broken down to create pebbles but interesting, don't you think, that some of these fossils have been perfectly preserved in the middle, right in the middle, of common beach pebbles? More likely, therefore, that the pebble was formed around them, rather than quite by chance a great big rock broke down to the point where the bit we saw just happened to contain a perfectly formed centralised fossil. And, as you must be aware, there are many millions of fossils found embedded inside pebbles.

Another interesting point: it is common to find two or three or even four pebbles moulded together. How on earth could this have happened unless the growth process, the

Reverse Theory, is true?

You sometimes find pebbles with holes in. Think about how this could have occurred. Imagine pebbles forming around a twig or a stick, imagine as the pebble grew and hardened, eventually the twig or stick would rot away; it would have to, due to its composition. So, you are left with a pebble with a hole in it. Again, how on earth could this have happened otherwise?

I would also like you to think about other growing rocks and structures on this planet, which may go some way to support my findings. Have you ever thought about stalagmites and stalactites?

STALAGMITES AND STALACTITES

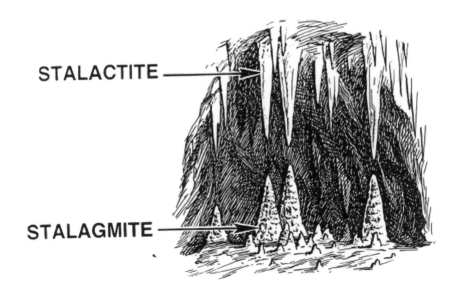

STALACTITE

STALAGMITE

Both these formations build up when water drips through rocks in a cave roof. The rocks themselves contain mineral deposits, namely calcite. It's this calcite along with other minerals that give stalagmites and stalactites their amazing colours.

With each drip, the water evaporates which leaves the calcite hanging on the cave roof in a sort of icicle, thus creating the stalactite. There are occasions, before the water evaporates, when it drips through onto the cave floor and builds a column of calcite which grows from the floor up, namely a stalagmite. Sometimes the stalactites and stalagmites grow up to meet each other. They then join and form a column. A stalactite 7 feet long takes about 4000 years to form.

It's interesting that the formation of stalagmites and stalactites can only occur when water hits the air. This is when the chemical transformation happens and the chemical makeup is altered, thus allowing the structures to form. What happens to sea water and tap water when it hits the air? Well, I would say, something similar. It's not just about the drying process it's about what happens to the water when it hits the air, the atmosphere. That's when the hardening process, the building and formation process of pebbles, is allowed to occur.

Backed up, once again, by the build up of lime scale in a kettle, which occurs when the kettle is devoid of water, here is another example of the chemical reaction needed to grow something, seemingly from nothing. And I hope this helps one to more easily understand what happens on our very own beaches.

Interestingly enough, when considering stalagmites and stalactites, we are talking about caves which are limestone caves. This stuff gets everywhere!

Limestone is a formation. It grows and changes shapes and starts off one texture and becomes another texture. It forms structures all over the world, in fact I'll come on to this in more detail a little later in the book. But for now, I just ask you to just think about the pebbles.

So, an interesting explanation of the Reverse Theory; some relevant examples of growth processes and, I hope, food for thought for you, the reader, to take away with you on your next journey to a pebbled beach or, indeed, your next journey through the science books and world wide web.

Isn't it just as plausible that beach pebbles actually get bigger from the continual slow application of debris and lime deposits, as it may be that pebbles become smaller from ongoing grinding against each other from the waves? Isn't it just as plausible that nature is in the process of building its own shoreline defences, as it is that nature is eroding its shores? I think so; I know so.

Isn't it completely conceivable that the moon has the job of ruling the tides to enable nature to build its own sea defences? Think about it: pebbles are a perfect defence against coastal erosion. We pollute the atmosphere and the rains wash the pollution back down to the ground, where eventually it finds its way into the sea, where the moon has the job of depositing this pollution onto our shores - I call it nature's toilet.

To keep a shoreline in place and stop coasts wearing away into the sea, pebbles are a wonderful natural defence. As the pebbles build, so the coastlines become safe against the powerful currents and crashing waves of our rougher seas. And so our shorelines remain intact.

The Reverse Theory does not ignore the fact that pebbles are simultaneously ground and broken down, especially in the winter; however this process is much slower than the building process.

If you look closely at broken pebbles you will see many multicoloured previous layers exposed within them, thus showing the evidence of a layered growth.

It would be a very valid question to ask about why shorelines are different in terms of their beaches. Why do some have pebbles and some sand? Sometimes even within the same vicinity.

The reason one shore has sand and another local or similar shore has pebbles is because long shore drift is in action. Long shore drift is where waves approach a shoreline at an angle, sand will zigzag its way across the shoreline giving no time for the tidemark to harden.

If you are one of those people who think there is more to life than meets the eye, then check out the pebbles. But remember the pebble theory is the complete opposite to what is taken to be a natural observation so it may take time to understand and, in turn, believe.

Perhaps the next step is for some bright spark (and they'd need to be bright and brave) to weigh pebbles. To take a pebbled shoreline as a field study; to spend some time studying it; watching and weighing specific pebbles as they increase in size. Because these pebbles will get microscopically heavier as time goes on. I don't know exactly how long a pebble takes to start its cycle but the last ice age, some ten thousand years ago, which rearranged shorelines and thus created new shorelines from scratch (more about this later in the book) would suggest it took ten thousand years to grow our current pebbles. What I do know for sure, is that it does happen, and now I'd like to see the geologists out there either prove me wrong, or prove the Reverse Theory right; if they dare.

Interestingly: I understand informal field studies have been undertaken to ascertain how quickly or slowly the erosion process was taking. Whilst this was done in the winter, where pebbles are under more stress from the environment, and therefore the study was slightly biased, it was discovered that some pebbles did in fact increase in size and weight.

The revelation of pebbles getting bigger is probably something you have never thought of before. You have quite probably just accepted the philosophies of the scientific authorities. However, new scientific discoveries are made every day that change the way we all look at science. Darwin himself was laughed at and publicly jeered when his theory was first published, but now it is deemed by the scientific majority to be accurate.

Pebbles getting bigger would surely seem impossible,

and anybody suggesting that they get bigger rather than smaller would arguably appear, at the least, if not stupid, mentally eccentric and potentially even mad. But then Copernicus, Galileo, Columbus, Darwin and many more were derided in many official quarters: Oxford, Cambridge, the complete science world and even the biblical world, when they first suggested an alternative view of the world.

Everyone's opinion is valid and we all have a voice and all deserve to have our say. It is my opinion that each and every one of us should look at the world around us and form our own philosophies through personal reasoning and contemplation. Free thinking will always be the road to discovery. By looking at the world with fresh eyes you will discover extraordinary things, then one day in the future you may well agree that the pebbles on the beach do indeed get bigger.

Stalgmites and stalactites

A beautiful shot depicting stalctite formation

As the 2 images illustrate, the calm tropical shore has a completely eroded shoreline whereas the rough violent shoreline shows very little in the way of erosion, surely this should be the other way around if rough seas were eroding our shores.

SAND

The Reverse Theory leaves a certain question unanswered: where does all the sand come from if not from ground down pebbles? The answer is simple: sand has come from the missing landscape from places like the Grand Canyon and canyons alike; and there are greater canyons and gorges under the sea which have all contributed. Clearly we have sand, along with its source: limestone, in abundance, and evidently the abundance of sand and the abundance of missing landscape appear to be somewhat of an equal. In other words, there seems to be as much missing landscape as there is sand.

I'd like to elaborate on the limestone point. Sand and

limestone are both made up of the same foundations, quartz, and both limestone and sandstone are classed as sedimentary rock, and sandstone is made of sand. Both limestone and sand contain quartz, silica, calcium carbonate, and feldspar, and both were once living sea-organisms. They are of the same origin and come from the world's canyons and gorges; they just ended up in different areas of the world. But, again, I'll cover this in more detail a little later in the book.

There is much to consider in terms of sand, pebbles and limestone. There is much to consider about the missing landscapes from, for example, the Grand Canyon and the Great Butts of Arizona. There is also much to consider about the masses of volcanoes and canyons above and below the ground and seas all over the world. These are topics to be opened up and explained. In order to do this, I want to continue with the process of explanation in the order I feel most fitting. The order I believe will make most sense, so that each piece of this book will fit perfectly with each other piece; giving you, the reader, a perfectly honed Reverse Theory.

HOW THE PYRAMIDS WERE BUILT

Now that I have explained the pebble phenomena, I want to continue our journey of discovery and reveal the secrets behind one of the biggest, and arguably the most intriguing, enigmas known to mankind: The Pyramids.

I quote from an encyclopaedia: 'Geology is the backbone of science. Everything that throws light on the history of Earth falls within the field of geology'. Geologists do not only study rocks for the rock itself but they study them for the information they give on the history of mankind; and now that we have found a weakness within the basic calculation behind geological time, deep time, we must consider where else our calculations could be at fault.

If we established a new train of thought regarding geology, or the timing thereof, using this as a foundation stone (pebble?) I'd like to introduce you to the second most important point of my book: one of the most intriguing mysteries this world has ever had to offer. I am going to reveal how the pyramids were built.

One of the world's great mysteries is solved here. Right on these very pages, before your very eyes.

It has long been a subject of intrigue and scrutiny. This mystery has baffled and mystified scientists and laymen through the ages. The pyramids, and their existence and meaning, are considered to be one of the most inexplicable conundrums that have ever beset mankind. How on earth were they built? How on earth did people physically cut, move, and get those huge great blocks of stone up so high? The same could be asked of similar limestone monuments and enigmas around the world; Stonehenge, Moai figures of Easter Island, Mayan Pyramids of Mexico and the Pyramids of South America, China and Asia, to name just a few.

Let's consider what the building conditions were at the time: I'm a carpenter and have been in the building trade all my life, and, even by today's standards and advanced building methods, the building of the pyramids would be a tall task, even with hydraulics. The sheer weight of one of the blocks is impossible to lift using manpower and animal power. And unlike today, with all our heavy plant machinery, all that was available at the time was: wood, copper, water, stone, animals and manpower.

Firstly, I'd like to take a look at commonly held views relating to the construction process. It is thought that the pyramid blocks were hewn from quarries using tools available at the time, namely stone and copper. Then the blocks were transported to the pyramid site using barges if the quarries were remote and wooden sledges when the quarries were local. You can see one such sledge, here.

A timber sledge (sled) made from cedar wood

The wheel would have been of little use during the Pyramid Age due to the heavy loads getting stuck in the soft ground of the sites. The sledges would have been the most appropriate means of carriage over-ground. They would have been dragged manually, presumably with the help of animals.

It is thought that some of the pathways were equipped with transverse wooden beams which lent some support to the sledges. Perhaps a lubricant of sorts would have been poured over the road to reduce the friction which would have undeniably occurred.

Interestingly, it is not understood for certain how the massive blocks were raised up to the height of the rising pyramid; it's thought that rubble off-cuts combined and packed with sand, formed the ramps that were used in the initial stages of building; but to build a ramp to lay the blocks at the top of the pyramid would have been a far greater task than building the pyramid itself.

There have been some extant ramps found at the sites of the Amenemhat and Senwosret pyramids at Lisht, as well as several other sites. The ramps, some of which have been found, disassembled, at pyramid sites, were made of brick or earth and rubble. They were understood to have been built upwards as the pyramid progressed upwards and then removed as the pyramid was finished downward.

At the beginning of work, the ramps are thought to have taken the form of an inclined plane but, in later stages, the configuration has always been a matter of sheer conjecture.

Egyptologists have long argued the possibilities and some believe that a straight, gently sloping, linear ramp was used. Others, that a spiralling ramp was constructed up the four sides of each pyramid. Of course the volume of the ramp would have to have exceeded the volume of the pyramid structure itself which suggests that the stones of the upper levels were placed using levers or a modified ramp of sorts.

Here we can see two photo's of inclined brick
construction ramps with the transverse timbers.

Taking an example of the Great Pyramid at Giza, as the upper reaches of the structure were such a small proportion of the total volume of the pyramid, extending a ramp up there seems to be impractical.

It is agreed that the Egyptians successfully completed the building of these massive, impressive, technically competent, advanced, structures; an amazing feat of architecture and construction, one unsurpassed throughout our history, I would say.

It is very hard to imagine that such feats would be possible, but the pyramids serve as a constant reminder that not only was it possible, it was very much achievable.

Interestingly, there are no written records explaining the process. Egyptologists have had to use remnants found at the construction sites to base their theories on; tangible archaeological evidence. However, some is open for debate as it is, quite simply, based upon theory.

Let's think about the people in question. Those who almost certainly arranged for construction to commence and who planned the projects: the Pharaohs. From mine and others' points of view, the Pharaohs were certainly not stupid and were deemed to be clever and relatively civilized. They were smart enough to somehow use complex calculation in their building projects, even though some Egyptologists may argue that they weren't aware of the calculation they were using. But, whatever they did, consciously or unconsciously, and however they did it, this is a clear indication that their whole projects were brilliantly planned and brilliantly executed, leaving nothing to chance.

I believe it is fair to suggest that they would not have built such gigantic structures unless they were relatively quick and straight forward to build and certainly not as mighty a task as some 'experts' would have us believe.

Granted, these structures took several years to construct, there was a lot of work involved, and, after all, we are talking mathematical precision here, a great feat of engineering, but why on earth would the Pharaohs have started constructing something which would take twenty years to build, with the view of creating a tomb for their leader? Surely that would be something that would be planned a little nearer, albeit still years, to their leader's death?

So, in terms of the current thought around the building of the Pyramids, I am not disputing any of the current construction theories. I am no geologist or Egyptologist, nor have I done more than read up on the subject and study photos and film of the sites in question. However, I would like to offer an additional piece of information, an additional theory, to explain the process in a much more understandable way.

Firstly, I have to say that copper is a soft metal and I have never quite been able to fathom how men of the time would have been able to use such inept tools for a project of such magnitude! It doesn't compute; and it also doesn't compute that science could even *suggest* copper tools would manage to cut such hard stone. I can understand that stone was used to assist the breaking and carving of the stone to be used as the building blocks, but to actually use such soft metal to achieve the final result is beyond me. Or rather, it was.

At the time of construction, the great blocks of stone,

which form our glorious pyramids, were quite simply a different texture. The stone that was carved by these supposedly inadequate copper tools was more like the consistency of the 'lightweight' breeze blocks that we find in today's builders' merchants.

Pyramids are formed of limestone and when limestone starts its life, it is soft. This is because, initially, it comes from marine organisms: dead sea life, which goes through a naturally occurring process to become incredibly hard. It in fact changes from one chemical composition to another, with various stages in between. So, at some point during the formation of limestone, from its initial soft state to its finished hardened state, there would come various stages of solidity. It was at a certain point during this process that the great blocks would have (and more importantly could have) been carved.

The hardening limestone would have dried easily in the hot Egyptian sun making the brittle consistency of the 'breeze block-type' blocks so much easier to work with. With each block drained of water, each block dried by the sun's rays, the forming limestone would have become lighter and easy to transport. Think how much easier this breaking and carving process would have been; how much lighter the blocks were and how comparatively easy the erection and construction process would have been.

We have accepted that giant tonnes of stone blocks were somehow, inexplicably, piled on top of each other with geometrical perfection. We have also accepted these vast structures as wonders of the world that will never be explained and we have accepted that this is just how it was, but can you see we don't have to just accept it, without explanation, anymore? Can you see how this process of hardening stone, hardening limestone, explains the mystery, and how it ties in with the forming and hardening pebbles?

The pyramids, as wondrous as they are, always have been and always will be, were not as hard to build as we have been led to believe. They were built using the most perfectly manageable stone, at a time in history when limestone was semi-cured: the half-way process between its original state and its current state.

Whilst the construction process would, I grant you, have been a magnificent and complex task; it is made so much more understandable when you consider the weight of the stone being so much less in volume. Et voila, there it is, questions and theories can be answered and explained. The feat can be seen as more easily achieved and our great structures, whilst no less amazing in their completion and accomplishment, have their construction mystery removed.

I find it intriguing that there hasn't been any known record of the building process of the pyramids. I find it very humbling that I was chosen to receive the truth about how these magnificent buildings were constructed. I am honoured to be able to share this information with you, even though writing this book was the most difficult and painful thing I have ever undertaken, and indeed hopefully ever will, within this life or subsequent lives.

I believe that the hardening of limestone has remained

undetected because our tools and cutting instruments have been getting stronger and sharper as time has gone on, and have therefore pushed to one side the questions about the implausibility of building the pyramids with cooper tools. When we think of building the pyramids, we think about building them with today's harder, sharper, and more effective hand tools. As the stone was getting harder and tougher our early copper tools were being replaced by bronze, and bronze was replaced by iron, and iron was replaced by steel. The whole project has therefore become blurred with theory and facts combined.

So, where does this leave us? This discovery alone is enough to warrant the publishing of this book, and a thousand other books from other sources will surely follow as a result. This in itself it is a major revelation in today's history. Knowing how the pyramids were built will open up science from within another dimension. There is however, more to it. I have to say there is more to the Reverse Theory that I could ever fully explain in a lifetime but the knowledge of the pyramids shows us something about the age of this planet. If the planet has been dated using geology, rocks, whether they be sand to pebbles or the dating of limestone in its hard state, what does it mean now that we know pebbles did not produce sand and the limestone used to build the pyramids was constructed when the stone was softer? Surely this means that dating rocks, radiometric dating, is flawed. Surely this means that we are basing the age of this planet on incorrect information. Of course, we can argue that meteorites have been dated using scientific methods, but what flaws lay there?

Young Earthers believe that there are a number of idiosyncrasies in the scientific reasoning in terms of what happens in our skies, our galaxies, so from my point of view it seems that the whole metric dating phenomenon has some basic errors in its foundations.

Limestone plays a large part in the Reverse Theory. We know that the pyramids are made from limestone, and I know that I've touched on this point previously, but, interestingly, although not surprisingly, cement is the hardening agent for concrete and cement is primarily made from limestone; the chief ingredient no less. Limestone is calcium carbonate and calcium carbonate is formed from marine organisms which is how limestone started in the first place. With this in mind, I'd now like to lead you on to another amazing case in point: The Grand Canyon; also formed of limestone. This now, undoubtedly, warrants closer inspection.

THE GRAND CANYON

This awesome wonder of the world is another factor that seemingly proves this planet is old. It apparently proves that deep time is a fact; a fact that is so ingrained it has become unquestionable (a bit like pebbles eroding to sand). It is said that the Grand Canyon is formed by the process of weathering and erosion. Erosion is the moving of material from one place to another.

Erosion is said to have occurred starting around seventeen million years ago.

From the size of the Grand Canyon, if you consider erosion, it is apparent that vast amounts of material were moved through the area, over periods of time, creating the canyons. No one is one hundred percent sure how this erosion took place but it's said that with repeated periods of flooding during previous periods of glaciations, dams formed by volcanism and their eventual breach, the susceptibility of certain rock layers in the canyon to be undercut by layers below them, and the ability of the Colorado River and its estuaries to transport the sediments, it was a process that did, in fact, occur.

I'm in obvious agreement that erosion of a sort took place but in the light of my previous findings, sand to pebbles, I suggest that we are missing some information.

The Grand Canyon has uncovered one of the most complete geological columns on the planet. These major exposures are said to range in age from the 2 billion year old Vishnu Schist at the bottom of the inner gorge, to the 230 million year old Kaibab limestone at the rim. Allegedly there is a gap of about one billion years between the stratum that is about 500 million years old and the lower level, which is about 1.5 billion years old. This indicates a period of erosion between two periods of deposition.

So, according to science, the earth's changing surfaces through ice ages, melting ice caps, volcanoes, general meteoric conditions and erosion, we have the formation of the Grand Canyon.

This process, as quoted, would have taken millions upon millions of years, in fact aeons.

I'm going to give you my take on this in a moment, but

firstly my questions are: where on earth, quite literally, did all the missing landscape from the Grand Canyon end up? Where did all the sea life from the moving Colorado River go? Where has all the dry earth, limestone, sand and debris gone to?

Perhaps, for a moment, we can go back to pebbles. Now we understand that they increase in size, we need to ask where the sand has come from that pebbles have grown from; after all sand is the seed that gives birth to a pebble, not the other way around.

I would suggest that the missing landscape from the Grand Canyon and other such canyons and gorges above and below the sea, e.g. the Great Buttes of Arizona, will have been responsible for much of this sand. For now, I'm taking the Grand Canyon as my case in point as I feel it's an excellent example and easy to understand.

Once upon a time the Grand Canyon wouldn't have been a canyon, but, instead, a much flatter landscape or, at least, certainly without the canyons we know and revere today. It was once, almost certainly, underwater, as it is made from limestone; limestone is a rock composed almost entirely of calcium carbonate, the remnant remains of what were once living sea organisms, therefore, just like in the case of the pyramids in the previous chapter, the vast plateau must have been soft at some stage.

I believe that during one of the earth's movements on its axis or perhaps after an ice age, possibly even both, the water would have dispersed from the plateau leaving a landscape of dying, drying, sea life.

In a nutshell: as this forming limestone dried it hardened to a texture that would crumble to sand, remember the breeze block effect I talked about previously? The drained water would have left the stone porous and an extremely hot drying sun would have virtually cooked the forming limestone leaving it dry and brittle, a texture that would crumble as the waters from the Colorado River and its estuaries, plus, of course, waters from the any major catastrophes, e.g. ice ages, flowed through it. As the waters carved through this dried landscape it would have crumbled into the gushing waters and dispersed itself around the world as sand.

Let's consider this in more detail: Planet Earth at that time would have been so different to the conditions we experience today. The abundance of limestone on our planet suggests the world was once covered by a primal soup of sea algae and sea organisms. Oceans would have been teaming and brimming with primitive sea life, like overzealous bacteria breeding at a rate faster than we can imagine, but at some stage when whatever catastrophe (ice ages, earth movement, comets, etc) befell the earth, the seas and landscapes would have shifted and both the land left behind and the missing landscape would have changed from one state to another: a transformation, a process within the science world, called 'metamorphism'. Remember: the same would have been happening all over the world, but for now the Grand Canyon is an excellent place for my explanation.

Much of the pre Grand Canyon landscape and sea life,

from the now shifted or dried up ocean, by whatever cause, would have been redistributed far and wide with a massive movement of water, possibly a melting ice age, or two. For the sea life these newly exposed waterless areas would have meant lethal conditions: conditions that saw the end of one era and the birth of another. These now dying sea creatures and plants would have been exposed to the different elements: air, wind and sun, with little or no water to survive in. Great mounds of dying sea organisms would simply have been left to dry and mutate, and this sea life, which is the backbone of limestone, would have started its slow process of fermenting and hardening; hardening to become limestone as we know it today. The new landscape, the pre Grand Canyon landscape, would have gradually formed.

The Canyon, in its current state, is formed of different layers of, amongst other components, this dead sea life (limestone) which, one could argue, has been formed with layers building on top of each other over many years.

After the shifting waters, there would have been different conditions, perhaps more ice ages, more waters moving, and more layers of dying sea life. We have no real way of knowing exactly what went on all these years back. Many of today's theories and so called facts are based upon speculation. But these layers are plain to see. And if we are to believe the scientists, it would seem that the formation of these layers of hardening limestone etc would indeed have taken millions of years.

According to science, the canyons, which now form the

Grand Canyon, were formed by the Colorado River and its estuaries gradually eroding these layers of limestone, over millions of years, to create valleys and canyons. So: millions of years to form and millions to erode, makes sense, yes? But why do we assume that the flowing water from the Colorado River, which reputedly carved out the Canyon as we see it today, was carving through solid rock? Why not consider the fact that it was making inroads through this forming limestone that hadn't fully hardened, either mud-like or brittle, depending on what stage the formation process was at?

I suggest that as more layers were building on top of each other and each layer was becoming denser at different rates, at the point at which the canyons were carved out these layers were still soft. Certainly soft enough to allow a great torrent of water mass to carve through them. I believe that whatever changes were happening to Planet Earth at the time, were happening frequently enough to build layers but for those layers not to harden fully.

I propose that there was a period of time without disruption of an ice age or the earth moving. I suggest there was an era without mass planetary water movement or the Colorado River bursting its banks. I believe that during that time the limestone layers would have been hardening at differing time scales; but at a point where none of it was hard enough to be considered rock, far from it. I then put forward the suggestion that a great flow of water rushed across this land with such a force that it caused the landscape to be

Sand under water and sand in the desert will remain sand
as there is no lapping seashore to change its consistency

*Some sand from under the oceans will gradually
be pushed up to the edges of beaches*

*Sand in the desert will remain sand as there is no
lapping seashore to change its consistency*

manoeuvred and cut through like a knife may cut through butter which is harder in some places than others. In fact firmer at the bottom than at the top, which would be the case with differing layers of limestone at different stages of their formation processes. Think about how the Grand Canyon looks today. The valleys, canyons and gorges are generally wider at the top than at the bottom. The bottom layers, the lower levels of the once hardening limestone, were harder than the top layers (due to the fact they were formed first and compressed) at the time of this final carving, and therefore harder to carve out, so more of the hardening limestone was left behind at the base.

This water movement would have spliced its way through the landscape and created the canyons, pretty much as we know them today. I strongly believe that the land that was removed from the landscape, in other words, the missing debris from the canyons, simply redistributed itself to other parts of the land and indeed under the sea as sand.

The debris under the oceans would have dispersed in part and be omnipresent as floating and settled debris. Some would have been food for plant and sea life and then, of course, we are left with sand. We know that sand and limestone are basically the same in their foundations, but in order for limestone to start forming, it needs the water removed. Sand however will remain sand, all the time it's under water.

Interestingly there is an abundance of limestone under the oceans which, I feel, strongly suggests the Earth's surface has been rearranged, after all, without this rearrangement, how on earth would the underwater limestone have formed? You need to add air and the atmosphere to the equation in order to bring about the chemical reaction causing dead sea life to become limestone.

If you think about this new theory of the Grand Canyon being softer when it was formed, then the time it took to form the geological column within the Canyon's layers was much less than the time science places upon it. Science says it took millions of years to form the rock then millions of years to erode it. But I say it didn't. I'm not an expert: I can't tell you exactly how long it took but, in laymen's terms, I do know that if the Canyon and other such structures and landscapes were reformed whilst relatively soft (certainly softer than present day limestone) the age of them would be much, much younger at the time of formation than we are led to believe.

Let's look at some other examples of relevant land formations.

If you were to draw a line from the top of one Butte to another (next page) you could see how much missing landscape has been removed and how much has crumbled to the base of the Butte.

We can see from the grooves on this landscape, again in Arizona, that when the water flowed it didn't hang around. This landscape has been carved out at great speed whilst the rock was soft and mud-like.

So to summarise: The Grand Canyon plateau and other such landscapes and canyons across the world, for example

The Great Buttes of Arizona is a fine example of missing landscape

the great Buttes of Arizona, were once soft, soft enough to be carved and formed by great torrents of rushing water. The flowing waters dispersed the still soft landscape carving out the canyons and thus leaving behind the mega structures we see today, structures that, over the years, have become hardened limestone. Obviously today's limestone is hard but the timing of the hardening process has now become questionable. Did, for example, the Colorado River carve its way through a hard rock, at the meandering pace that we are told and live by today, i.e. millions of years, or did it carve its way through a soft rock, in a similar way that water would carve through mud?

Pebbles and the building of the pyramids would suggest the latter.

The missing landscape from the canyons would have journeyed across the lands to its new positions, some of this missing landscape would have ended up forming sandstone cliffs, hills and other land masses which, over time, would have hardened and become the landscapes we see and love today. Much of the loose material would have swept across our planet and found its final resting place under the seas and oceans, and of course formed our deserts and beaches. With the ebb and flow of the daily tides, gradually ridges of this sand would have been pushed up to the edges to create the world's first beaches, the final resting places. And many of these shorelines would witness another great phenomenon: the birth of the beach pebble.

WHAT IS THE CORRECT AGE OF PLANET EARTH?

What we must reflect upon is our indoctrinated beliefs of deep time and indeed the fossil records. We must consider both scientific principles compressed within a much shorter time span. Beach pebbles tell us we have a flaw within the timing of geology whilst the building of the pyramids tell us the limestone blocks were more manageable six thousand years ago, certainly a different texture than today.

The humble beach pebble, the building of the pyramids, sand, and the formation of the Grand Canyon and other canyons alike, all share a common theme: that this planet has been severely over estimated, time-wise.

It would seem the pre-Grand Canyon limestone plateau was much softer than previously thought, and I would suggest this was only a few thousand years before the pyramids were built. If the limestone blocks were at a perfect texture for building pyramids, six thousand years ago, it would be prudent to think that the forming stone was a wet mud-like texture not so many years previously. Even if the hardening times of limestone were different around the globe (due to different environmental conditions) there would still be a huge argument to say science has got it wrong, geology is flawed, and that Planet Earth is a young earth, not an old one.

In terms of putting an actual age on our planet we have

to look at the pebbles again. Rather than asking 'How long did it take a pebbled beach to look like a sandy beach?' - The question is: 'How long did a sandy beach take to look like a pebbled beach?' which according to the last ice age is just over ten thousand years ago. A thawing ice age would have altered all shorelines and created new ones, where pebbles would have started forming. About ten thousand years ago an ice age covered most of the northern hemisphere. It is common knowledge that a mile thick ice sheet covered Manchester, Birmingham and North London. When it melted, this receding ice sheet, this ebb, would have started a massive flood, a rearrangement of land and water and clearly have started the shoreline formation process from scratch.

Let's now look at the thawing process involved and how it affects our thoughts and our understanding of the Earth's age. Masses upon masses of the planet's melting ice would have caused torrents of water to shift around the planet: Tsunamis in abundance. Shorelines would have formed and reformed. Landscapes that hadn't been under water would have been covered. Seas would either have increased their levels or may have shifted to disclose new land. Let's face it; as no one was around at the time, none of us knows exactly what happened. Regardless of the exact details, new shorelines would have been created through ice ages or the planet moving or wobbling on its axis, which it does every so often; thus sand would have moved from different places on the globe. Sand that was under the sea would have been exposed and now new sandy beaches would have been born. Like I said, the last ice age was reportedly about ten thousand years ago, so that is when our most recent upheaval happened.

Once the new shorelines settled you would find that in rougher, more polluted seas, I'll take the English Channel as an example, the incoming tides would have carried more debris, more pollution, with more particles to be distributed over the shores. You'll find pebbled beaches where the tides and waves are stronger and the pollution is greater. These are the beaches that produce pebbles, as opposed to the silently softly lapping, less polluted shorelines of, for example, the Caribbean.

The Reverse Theory cannot profess to ascertain the correct age of our planet but would say deep time is a figment of our imagination. Science can find out the true age by analysing the drying and hardening process of the limestone that built the pyramids. Many of the early pyramids collapsed under their own weight, like the earlier Bent Pyramid located 40 kilometres south of Cairo, which is a unique example of early pyramid development. Calculating the time between building those soft pyramids and the great pyramid at Giza, which is a strong rock hard structure, would give the time limestone took to harden. Then it's just a case of working out the mathematics in reverse, right back to the Grand Canyon and the production of sand.

Reanalysing The Grand Canyon and the geological column within, will give us a better understanding of the sequence of events that led to its formation, the possible age of the planet and life upon it. We can then fill in the missing pieces of the jigsaw, unanswered mysteries can be solved, and geologists and physicists can recalculate their mathematics behind radiometric dating.

DINOSAURS

I believe that dinosaurs were around a lot more recently that previously thought due to their demise being brought about by the hardening of limestone; the same limestone that went to forming the Grand Canyon, and at a similar time.

Dinosaurs were creatures of gigantic size and obviously ate accordingly. Sea life, or forming limestone, was everywhere in abundance; we must conclude therefore that they ate a lot of it. Imagine what would have happened when this sea life was drying out and hardening, no more food! The sea life would have been drying out and in the process of becoming limestone so the food source for the dinosaurs would literally have ceased.

We know that limestone comes from dead sea creatures; this is one of nature's clever idiosyncrasies, so allow yourself to think of this in real terms. Once upon a time, before it was limestone, it was food. Therefore, it would have supported the dinosaurs for years, encouraging their existence, whereas the hardening of this forming limestone, this sea life, would have brought about their demise. I believe that this would have been the case, rather than the highly controversial theory of a catastrophic meteorite impact causing the dinosaur's extinction. Of course, these supposed meteoric impact craters do exist, that's plain to see, but I suggest that the craters were formed by bubbling mud pools from within the earth, rather than impact. This is another example of the Reverse Theory's opposite approach to explanation. In this case, it is matter pushing out from within, rather than matter pushing in from without. The without, in this case, being space.

RT suggests these craters are the result of a bubbling surface coming up from within the earth's core, rather than impact craters from meteorites hitting the earth. If these are meteorite craters it seems strange they are all direct hits with no sign of meteorites hitting from acute angles or the meteorite itself.

The dinosaurs give us an interesting case for helping us to put an age to the planet. Many dinosaur remains have been found encased in limestone, as have their footprints. We know that this limestone started soft and became hard so, with this knowledge, we can put a date to the limestone in question and hence an age to the dinosaur remains; thus putting a date to when the dinosaurs were alive. How long did that limestone take to harden? We can see that the dinosaurs would have been alive shortly before limestone started to set like concrete.

Working on my previous revelations on the formation timing of limestone, I would suggest that the dinosaurs became extinct, not 65 million years ago (the indoctrinated KT Boundary – the mass dinosaur extinction)...but perhaps closer to 65 thousand years ago. This is, of course, an assumption of timing on my part, but considering the formation process and the flaw in geology, I feel strongly that this is something for geologists to consider.

I sincerely believe that life upon this planet has been severely over estimated, time-wise, and I believe that the dinosaurs, along with the limestone surrounding them and their demise, are another previously missing piece of the puzzle which will now help us ascertain the correct age of Planet Earth.

DESCENT & DEMISE
OF EARLIER MAN

With geology undoubtedly flawed, the origins of mankind now become somewhat questionable. We find that the scientific foundations, upon which we base and stack all our philosophies and theories, are not completely accurate, and the theory of evolution is not as logical as we were led to believe. Given the new time scale which is revealed through the Reverse Theory, unless evolution worked at supersonic speed, it could not have happened in the way it has been reported. Quite simply, there would not have been enough time to mould modern man from a monkey, let alone from absolutely nothing!

If it becomes common belief that the planet is not old enough to warrant the theory of evolution as we know it, it will beg the question: where does the primate family come from if not from evolution? This is a similar question to 'where does sand come from if not from ground down pebbles'. Something to consider: if the planet is not old enough to support the theory of evolution, where do we all come from?

Calculating these new facts will continue for decades and, I believe, will eventually conclude that mankind could not have derived from primates.

I suggest that rather than mankind evolving from apes it is, quite simply, the other way around; the reverse: primates and, indeed, other mammals are extracted from mankind.

Considering that the Reverse Theory is one for polar opposites, this revelation will be no different. However, if you cannot accept sand to pebbles, or relate to how the pyramids were built, or the fact that sand comes from our missing landscapes, or the hardening process of limestone bringing about the dinosaur's demise, or the planet not being old enough to warrant the theory of evolution, there is no way you could accept that primates were once human, as opposed to humans once being primates.

This is perhaps the toughest one to call and certainly a tough one to understand but bear with me while I put my thinking to you.

It is common knowledge that our planet has experienced a number of catastrophes during its lifetime: thousands of erupting volcanoes, many ice ages, perhaps the planet has even shifted or wobbled on its axis a few times. Some catastrophes would have been before man was alive and some would have been after his arrival on this planet. It would have been one such disaster which left mankind in a state of demise. I believe that at some point in our history, part of the human race took a turn for the worst and became part of the animal kingdom rather than the other way around. In essence, due to the world's catastrophes and environment, mankind would have entered a living hell and lived like an animal. After this it would have simply been a matter of time before humans became animal, certainly some of mankind, cross-breeding through the spectrum of the animal kingdom. I'm going to explain this in more detail and I believe that the pebble phenomenon will help shed light on the subject.

The mass amounts of pebbles that now lay at the bottom of the oceans, the ones dredged up for making concrete, play a very important role in this revelation and I hope will back up my theory. These pebbles under the sea have been formed by layers upon layers of pollution; they would have been formed on a tidal shoreline, as explained in the chapter about pebbles. There can be no doubt that where these pebbles now lay must have been part of a shoreline themselves. They would have formed their very own beaches, which mean those shorelines would have once been exposed.

The oceans have moved; the Earth's surface has changed. The now hidden shorelines would once have had their own tides and would have started as sandy shores, and their pebbles would have grown just like any other pebbled beach. Therefore, it's safe to say, at some point in our history, the planet has experienced an almighty flood beyond the realms of our current understanding; a flood that would have shifted shorelines and replaced seas; a flood of such magnitude that the whole of the Earth would have been affected by it; and that includes mankind.

A little piece of information that may serve to back up my point here: there is evidence that about 7450 years ago the land gap between North Africa and Gibraltar, i.e. the straits of Gibraltar, was once a waterfall a thousand times greater than Niagara Falls, which shows that a significant change in the water in that area would have occurred.

Any flood that could fill up the Mediterranean, carve

out the Grand Canyon, leave an abundance of sea life out of water to become limestone, flatten the forests causing massive dams of wood (i.e. our coal fields), would have been colossal; something on a scale well beyond our comprehension, and caused devastation on an unprecedented scale.

As I've alluded to previously, the flood could have been caused by many different scenarios, perhaps the planet wobbled on its axis, or an ice age may have been the cause, either way, if both ice caps were suddenly at the equator, melting, and moving back again towards the poles, which is a likely scenario, water would have been exploding across this planet with such a force, that devastation would have ensued.

Another possible explanation for the Earth's rearrangement is the dried up waterways on the planet Mars. They suggest that the Sun expanded or moved closer to us, which would have caused conditions on our planet to change drastically.

Whatever happened, I believe that the upheaval would have brought about terrific mayhem on the planet, not just massive floods. I believe that Planet Earth would have been a mass of catastrophes. Volcanoes would have erupted, earthquakes would have shaken the core, noxious gases would have emanated through every orifice and crater, the tidal waves would have crashed through each and every continent and survival would have been incredibly hard. I believe that the Earth's atmosphere would have been a clouded mass of black, gassy, fog which would have potentially blocked out the sun for years. Think about the effect that some large industrial chimneys have on the atmosphere; imagine that multiplied and multiplied. The atmosphere would have been seriously affected and the poisonous gasses and fog would have hung like great sheets in the air. Conditions for mankind would have been terrible; truly hellish. To survive in these conditions, one can only imagine would have been life threatening, and finding food would have proved extremely difficult and potentially brought about much fighting, even warring; survival of the fittest.

I believe that it was at this stage that mankind took one of two directions: those fitter and stronger would have survived as mankind but those more savage would have literally turned into savages and bred like savages. Savages breeding more savages will eventually live like animals rather than humans. If you think about evolution in reverse, why not? If man can rise from ape, according to science, why not the other way around? To me it makes perfect sense. A being, any being, will change itself to survive within its surroundings; chameleonize. Natural survival skills within unnatural surroundings will have brought about a war with the elements, with other beings and animals and all in all a chaotic turmoil of an existence. In this case a terrible Hell on earth.

Today we have different people skilled in different skill sets, and it would have been the same back then. Some would have been more intellectually agile and others more physically fit; some both. The strongest in reason and strength and

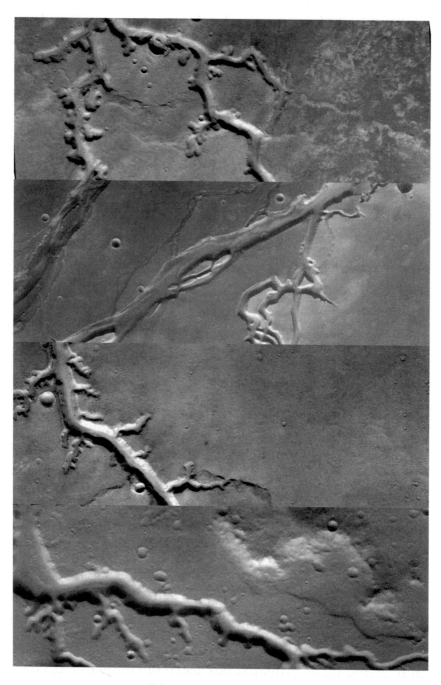

Waterways of planet Mars

nurture would have survived as human beings and perhaps those with more tribal instincts, would have acted out a more savage existence and become, as I said, like savages. Can you see how a savage would become more savage-like over the ages? Can you see how some of mankind could have, in effect, devolved? But really, it's not devolving; it is merely evolving in a different direction. Like sand to pebble, no-one has ever considered the opposite to evolution; the evolution as we have been taught it.

Seeing as the Reverse Theory deals mainly in opposites, I wouldn't want this to be any different.

I said I would explain where Hell was, and I believe I have. Hell was a place on Earth which mankind experienced, many, many, thousands of years ago. I believe it was this Hell on earth that caused man to not only evolve into the animal kingdom, but also at a great speed. I believe it is easier to go down to a more savage state than it is to evolve from a savage state; hence, as opposed to the commonly taught evolution, there would have been enough time for this process to happen within the new time frames of a younger Earth. At the same time the rest of mankind would have evolved as normal; man becoming more evolved man. The more savage beings, took the journey to the animal kingdom. We know there were once Neanderthal and Cavemen roaming the Earth, and I believe we all went down to that level then some carried on down to the animal kingdom; basically they went past the point of return. Personally, I believe there is a case to suggest we not only ended up as primates, but also other animals too; cross-breeding into the animal kingdom as a whole.

Interestingly, the ancient Egyptians depicted half man half animal monuments, statues, tombs and hieroglyphics; one well known monument is, of course, the Sphinx. I seriously wonder sometimes whether the Egyptians witnessed or were witnessing this fall in mankind!

You can see some examples of half man half beast, here, and I've included some more in-depth information towards the end of the book.

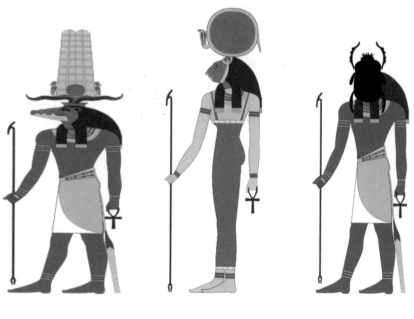

Sobk/Crocodile   *Sekhmet/Lion*   *Khepri/Scarab Beetle*

Charles Darwin offered up the theory of evolution and it was just that, a theory. Based on this theory, scientists, geologists, zoologists, biologists etc, took his theoretical ideas

and made the assumption, again, that the planet must be old, and did their research with deep-time in mind. If he had seen his theory the correct way around, in reverse, those men of science would have based their research on a young planet.

Science is built on facts, first and foremost, and, if one of those facts at the very grass roots of science is wrong, it would cast a cloud over all that followed. I believe that the Reverse Theory has successfully challenged the foundations of mankind and this planet and we have now been given the tools with which to work out the true age of the Earth, as well as understand the truth about evolution.

I believe, without question, that the whereabouts of Hell has now been explained, which I hope will offer some relief when considering the afterlife. God forbid some people are still thinking we are destined to Hell and damnation, fire and brimstone. I believe that those times were on Earth, and are now over and forgotten; thankfully.

SUMMARY
MY 15 MINUTES OF FAME
(OK.... MY 5 MINUTES OF FAME!)

I'd like to summarize the Reverse Theory by sharing with you a great experience, which left me feeling on top of the world! I sometimes listen to talk radio and one night about midnight I was in bed listened to Talk Sport radio 'The James Whale Show' where he posed a particular question which made my ears prick up and my heart skip a beat. He was asking about Hell. Specifically asking his listeners: does it exist and, if so, where is it? I thought to myself I know exactly where Hell is and I knew I had to call him. It was the first and last time I've ever done such a thing but the call to air my Reverse Theory was too great to ignore.

Within a few minutes I had got through. James is a bit of a gee-up merchant but his immediate banter went straight over my head; I wasn't going to rise to his bait. He was babbling about something petty, trying to be funny and make his show stand out from the rest but I was determined to get my point across so I moved quickly on, talking over him. .

'James!' I said in a loud voice, 'you wanted to know here Hell is'

His reply was: 'Well, do you know where Hell is'?

I thought: this is my chance to put my views on national radio. I was feeling a bit mischievous as I had the house to myself and it was my chance to get my controversial theories across. Here was a platform to voice my discoveries and to advertise my website.

I replied: 'Yes I do. It was a place that existed a long time ago but the door is firmly shut, it doesn't exist anymore, it's gone; it's finished.'

He asked me to explain in more detail.

I replied, words to the effect: 'It was the saddest, vilest, grimiest place you could ever imagine. Awful, disgusting, terrible; words cannot describe this place. It was the saddest place one could ever imagine.' I went into one and got quite carried away with my description as, to me, Hell really was the saddest place on Earth; the worst place that anyone could set foot in; a place of no escape. It sickens me to the stomach just thinking about it. I went on to repeat: 'The door to Hell is firmly shut; shut forever. It doesn't exist anymore; it is over, finished, gone.'

James was quite intrigued: 'But where is it?' he urged in a tone reminiscent of fiction, probably thinking that nobody could ever answer such a question.

I laughed and replied: 'To tell you where hell is or, more to the point, where it was, I would first have to explain how the pyramids were built!'

'Can you?' he replied in a high pitched sarcastic tone, clearly quite surprised.

'Yes!' I said. 'Yes I can.'

The line went silent for a second. I assumed at this point James had gone from humouring me to being pretty intrigued.

'Go on then', he encouraged.

I was amazed. This was my chance, this was my time, and I now had a platform from which to speak. I had an audience.

'Can I?' I asked. I couldn't quite believe my luck.

James confirmed that I should continue.

I began to talk, albeit with a slight stutter.

'OK, um, well, to cut a beautiful long story short, when science calculated the age of this planet one of the first equations they used was the principle of erosion: i.e. how long it took nature to make all the sand in the world. In other words: how long it took a pebbled beach to look like a sandy beach; solid rock to boulders to pebbles to sand.'

To make sure he was listening I asked him if he knew what I meant, he agreed and replied: 'Yes I understand.'

I continued: 'Well that theory is wrong, very wrong. Pebbles are formed by the principle of tidemark not by the principle of erosion.' I told him that the tide comes in and leaves a layer of crap from the water on the shore, the tide goes out and then the sun dries the crap forming a layer which hardens. I felt funny using the word 'crap' on national radio but needs must in the short space of time I had.

I explained that a cluster of four or five grains of sand eventually stick together through this process and form divots; then the incoming tide fills those divots, and gradually pebbles are formed by a layer by layer growth process. Grains of sand become grit, grit becomes gravel, gravel becomes shingle, and so-on and so-forth.

He seemed to understand where I was coming from but then asked: 'But, um, but, how does that explain how the pyramids were built?'

I hastily replied: 'because science has miscalculated the age of the planet, it means that when the pyramids were built, the limestone they were made from was a different texture than it is today: it was soft, light; similar to the lightweight building blocks of today.' I said: 'You could cut it with a piece of stick let alone a piece of copper which was what the Egyptians tools were made from.

I explained: 'You could 'float up' (builders' term) the blocks with a block of wood, like plasterers use when rendering a house.

I asked if he knew what I meant by lightweight building blocks, he replied quite confidently: 'Yes I do.'

I explained that the blocks were just like that, light and very manageable, a bit like dried up cuttlefish that you find washed up on the seashore.

I felt he was warming to me a little and that this was, in fact, quite acceptable. Without dwelling on it, he asked: 'But how does that explain where Hell is?'

I replied: 'Because they have miscalculated the age of the planet, when the Grand Canyon was formed, by the way...' I added...' that is where a large amount of the world sand has come from, a catastrophe hit this planet beyond the realms of all understanding and it was at that time when mankind took a turn for the worse. No longer were they living in the land of plenty but in a place that can only be described as Hell. The conditions on this planet were a living nightmare: floods and storms, and thousands of erupting volcanoes holding deathly smog within the atmosphere. The Sun was blocked out for many years and in these conditions, many humans became like savages and acted like savages. They became like animal and many did, indeed, deteriorate down to animal. Some crossed the point of no return and crossbred into the spectrum of the animal kingdom: first to the family of the primates, then dogs, bears, horses, penguins, dolphins, etc,' I explained. 'That is where Hell was: the point of no return,' I concluded.

'After all' I went on, 'if we can come up from apes as is commonly thought, then I'm sure we could do it in reverse … and, I don't doubt, a lot quicker. Take for instance the whale: a mammal that had limbs clearly showing they were once walking the land. Basically, we have understood evolution backwards. We didn't come from apes, mankind became apes, but not just apes, other animals too; and we, the lucky ones, are now heading back to our former glory, perhaps to live to one thousand years old like the good book suggests; like Adam who lived to be 930 years old.' I concluded: 'So, what I'm saying is: Hell was in fact a place on Earth where humans deteriorated down to animal and stayed as such. We are really talking Hell on Earth. But that has all changed now, and life has moved on and the door to this place is firmly shut,' I said, feeling elated at having told my story, albeit in a brief way. And at this point I plugged the Reverse Theory … It would have been silly not to!

I have to laugh at this point because James Whale said,

and I quote: 'Chris, you are as mad as a March Hare!' and promptly went in to the commercial break.

THE AFTERLIFE

I am now certain that evolution did not occur and with that being the case, I lean far more strongly to the creation point of view: intelligent design.

If Hell has been found, i.e. man to animal, then in my opinion it seems reasonable to assume that Heaven must also be a place on Earth. I believe we are part of a developing Heaven; a place of reincarnation. I would suggest, in light of this, when you die, you don't die at all. Your soul must reincarnate. It must rejuvenate itself and come back again.

You sometimes hear about people who go under hypnosis and regress to another life. They can relate to a world gone by. Some speak other languages unbeknown to them while others tell tales of another life in another country. This would strongly suggest that reincarnation is a fact of life.

So, if Heaven isn't a different dimension, and really it's a place on Earth, and this is a developing heaven, then surely it is our responsibility to create it in the perfect way. We need to focus our thoughts and minds and hearts on the perfect Heaven, the perfect world so what do we want from Heaven. What do we want to see; to create; to experience. We are building this. It's up to us.

There are some wonderful sights on this planet and every time I see a beautiful sight (mainly on television) I always ask myself 'What would I like to see in the afterlife? What would I like to see if I went to heaven? As I mentioned earlier, if you are spiritually inclined you are in for a real treat. You'll be able to peep through into the unknown because life, it seems, is a continuum, ie, when you die, you don't, you can never stop thinking. What you do with those thoughts is up to you, but it seems however, you take with you your soul and what is in your heart, not what is in your head or brain but what is strongly rooted in your subconscious, your mind.

You would also have to take on board the sacrifices that went before you, the sacrifice of your fellow man that made up the animal kingdom and hence understand the true meaning of sacrifice. The Crucifixion is the supernatural or philosophical or even metaphorical way of telling us that to build heaven sacrifices had to be made. There is no other way, there was no other choice.

I hope the Reverse Theory has made you think. I hope it has opened your eyes to some alternative thinking and some alternative possibilities. I sincerely hope you have kept an open mind and are willing to consider and hopefully accept what I believe to be some of the most important new truths that this planet, this race, has ever been given. I look forward to witnessing the effects of the words included in the Reverse Theory as, like any new revelations channelled down into the human mind, they were clearly meant to be received, understood and integrated.

My wish for you is that you keep your mind and heart open to new information; aim to steer clear of rigid thinking and always be willing to accept the unchartered with interest, enthusiasm and love. There is so much to learn, so much information on offer in this life, so much to experience, so why not be open to it all; you never know what it might lead to.

There now follows some more in depth information on areas covered in the Reverse Theory. These span the Egyptian man/beast examples, the arguments for a young earth, religion, and science and some information about publishers and agents I've sent my work to.

Much of this will be in the words of others, and I offer it up here simply to complete the picture from all angles. It may be interesting for you to understand the perspectives of others so you can make a comparison and decide for yourself your own truth; you may, however, decide that the previous information is enough. That is your choice, as is everything in your life.

EXAMPLES OF EGYPTIAN ART

Examples of Egyptian Art depicting half man half animal included the the *Head of Anubis* as in the exampe left.

Thoth/Ibis   Amon-ra   Horus/Falcon

Other deity's represented by animals are: Ptah the *Bull* - Thoth the *Ibis/Baboon* – Amun the *Ram* - Horus/Ra the *Falcon/Hawk* - Anubi the *Jackal/Dog* - Sobek the *Crocodile* -

Hathor the *Cow* - Sekhmet the *Lion* - Nekhbet the *Vulture* - Ejo or Wadjet the *Egyptian Cobra* - Khepri the *Scarab Beetle* - Geb – *Egyptian Goose*. And of course we have the Sphinx.

British Museum - The judgement of the dead in the presence of Osiris from Thebes 19th Dynasty, around 1275 BC

This is an excellent example of one of the many fine illustrations from the *Book of the Dead*. The scene reads from left to right. To the left, Anubis brings Hunefer into the judgment area. Anubis is also shown supervising the judgment scales. Hunefer's heart, represented as a pot, is being weighed against a feather, the symbol of Maat, the established order of things, in this context meaning 'what is right'. The ancient Egyptians believed that the heart was the seat of the emotions, the intellect and the character, and thus represented the good or bad aspects of a person's life. If the heart did not balance with the feather, then the dead person was condemned to non-existence and consumption by the ferocious 'devourer', the strange beast shown here which is part-crocodile, part-lion, and part-hippopotamus. However, as a papyrus devoted to ensuring Hunefer's continued existence in the Afterlife is not likely to depict this outcome, he is shown to the right, brought into the presence of Osiris by his son Horus, having become 'true of voice' or 'justified'. This was a standard epithet applied to dead individuals in their texts. Osiris is shown seated under a canopy, with his sisters Isis and Nephthys. At the top, Hunefer is shown adoring a row of deities who supervise the judgement.

Below are other illustrations from the book of the dead showing human/animal examples:

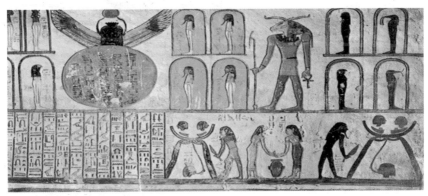

A YOUNG EARTH PERSPECTIVE

I'd like to thank www.answeringeneses.org for their helpful information. You will find references for all the information here listed at the end of this book.

From a Young Earthers perspective you can see that even before the revelations in the Reverse Theory, scientific proof of the age of this planet has been successfully challenged.   Here   are   fourteen   natural phenomena which conflict with the evolutionary idea that the universe is billions of years old. The following items are evidence against the evolutionary time scale. Much more evidence for a young earth exists but I have chosen these items for brevity and simplicity. Some of the items on this list can be reconciled with the old age view only by making a series of improbable and unproven assumptions; others can fit in only with a recent creation.

1. Many strata are too tightly bent.

In many mountainous areas, rock strata thousands of feet thick are bent and folded into tight hairpin shapes and bends. The conventional geologic time scale says these formations were deeply buried and solidified for hundreds of millions of years before they were bent. Yet the folding occurred without cracking, with radii so small that the entire formation had to be still wet and un-solidified when the bending occurred. This implies that the folding occurred less than thousands of years after deposition.

2. Not enough Stone Age skeletons.

Evolutionary anthropologists now say that Homo sapiens existed for at least 185,000 years before agriculture began, during which time the world population of humans was roughly constant, between one and ten million. All that time they were burying their dead, often with artefacts. By that scenario, they would have buried at least eight billion bodies. If the evolutionary time scale is correct many of the supposed eight billion skeletons should still be around (certainly the buried artefacts). Yet only a few thousand have been found. This implies that the Stone Age was much shorter than evolutionists think, perhaps only a few hundred years.

3. Agriculture is too recent.

The usual evolutionary picture has men existing as hunters and gatherers for 185,000 years during the Stone Age before discovering agriculture less than 10,000 years ago. Yet the archaeological evidence shows that Stone Age men were as intelligent as we are. It is very improbable that none of the eight billion people mentioned in the item above should discover that plants grow from seeds. It is more likely that men were without agriculture for a very short time after this Flood, if at all.

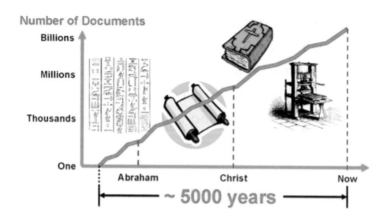

Number of Documents

Billions

Millions

Thousands

One

Abraham   Christ   Now

~ 5000 years

4. History is too short.

According to evolutionists, Stone Age Homo Sapiens existed for 190,000 years before beginning to make written records about 4,000 to 5,000 years ago. Prehistoric man built megalithic monuments, made beautiful cave paintings, and kept records of lunar phases. Why would he wait two thousand centuries before using the same skills to record history? Meaning the biblical time scale is much more likely.

5. Biological material decays too fast.

Natural radioactivity, mutations, and decay degrade DNA and other biological material decay rapidly. Measurements of the mutation rate of mitochondrial DNA recently forced researchers to revise the age of "mitochondrial Eve" from a theorized 200,000 years down to possibly as low as 6,000 years. DNA experts insist that DNA cannot exist in natural environments longer than 10,000 years, yet intact strands of DNA appear to have been recovered from fossils allegedly much older: Neanderthal bones, insects in amber, and even from dinosaur fossils. Bacteria allegedly 250 million years old apparently have been revived with no DNA damage. Soft tissue and blood cells from a dinosaur have astonished experts.

6. Fossil radioactivity shortens geologic "ages" to a few years.

Radio-halos are rings of colour formed around microscopic bits of radioactive minerals in rock crystals. They are fossil evidence of radioactive decay. "Squashed" Polonium-210 radio-halos indicate that Jurassic, Triassic, and Eocene formations in the Colorado plateau were deposited within months of one another, not hundreds of millions of years apart as required by the conventional time scale. "Orphan" Polonium-218 radio-halos, having no evidence of their mother elements, imply accelerated nuclear decay and very rapid formation of associated minerals.

7. Too much helium in minerals.

Uranium and thorium generate helium atoms as they decay to lead. A study published in the Journal of Geophysical Research showed that such helium produced in zircon crystals in deep, hot Precambrian granite rock has not had time to escape. Though the rocks contain 1.5 billion years worth of nuclear decay products, newly-measured rates of helium loss from zircon show that the helium has been leaking for only 6,000 (+/- 2000) years. This is not only evidence for the youth of the earth, but also for episodes of greatly accelerated decay rates of long half-life nuclei within thousands of years ago, compressing radioisotope timescales enormously.

8. Too much carbon 14 (C14) in deep geologic strata.

With their short 5,700-year half-life, no C14 atoms should exist in any carbon older than 250,000 years. Yet it has proven impossible to find any natural source of carbon below Pleistocene (Ice Age) strata that does not contain significant amounts of C14, even though such strata are supposed to be millions or billions of years old. Conventional C14 laboratories have been aware of this anomaly since the early 1980s, have striven to eliminate it, and are unable to account for it. Lately the world's best such laboratory which has learned during two decades of low-C14 measurements how not to contaminate specimens externally, under contract to creationists, confirmed such observations for coal samples and even for a dozen diamonds, which cannot be contaminated in situ with recent carbon. These constitute very strong evidence that the earth is only thousands, not billions, of years old.

9. Not enough mud on the sea floor.

Each year about 20 billion tons of dirt and rock from

the continents are deposited on to the ocean floor. This material accumulates as loose sediment on the hard basaltic (lava-formed) rock of the ocean floor. The average depth of all the sediment in the whole ocean is less than 400 meters. The main way known to remove the sediment from the ocean floor is by plate tectonic subduction. That is, sea floor slides slowly (a few cm/year) beneath the continents, taking some sediment with it. According to secular scientific literature, that process presently removes only 1 billion tons per year. As far as

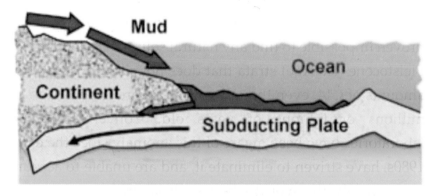

Rivers and dust storms dump mud into the sea much faster than plate tectonic subduction can remove it.

anyone knows, the other 19 billion tons per year simply accumulate. At that rate, erosion would deposit the present mass of sediment in less than 12 million years. Yet according to evolutionary theory, erosion and plate subduction have been going on as long as the oceans have existed, an alleged three billion years. If that were so, the rates above imply that the oceans would be massively choked with sediment dozens of kilometres deep. An alternative young earthers (creationist) explanation is that erosion from the waters of the Genesis flood running off the continents deposited the present amount of sediment within a short time about 5,000 years ago.

10. Not enough sodium in the sea.

Every year, rivers and other sources dump over 450 million tons of sodium into the ocean. Only 27% of this sodium manages to get back out of the sea each year. As far as anyone knows, the remainder simply accumulates in the ocean. If the sea had no sodium to start with, it would have accumulated its present amount in less than 42 million years at today's input and output rates. This is much less than the evolutionary age of the ocean, three billion years. The usual reply to this discrepancy is that past sodium inputs must have been less and outputs greater. However, calculations that are as generous as possible to evolutionary scenarios still give a maximum age of only 62 million years. Calculations for many other seawater elements give much younger ages for the ocean.

11. Galaxies wind themselves up too fast.

The stars of our own galaxy, the Milky Way, rotate about the galactic centre with different speeds, the inner ones rotating faster than the outer ones. The observed rotation speeds are so fast that if our galaxy were more than a few hundred million years old, it would be a featureless disc of stars instead of its present spiral shape. Yet our galaxy is supposed to be nearly 10 billion years old. Evolutionists call this "the winding-up dilemma," which they have known about for fifty years. They have devised many theories to try to explain it, each one failing after a brief period of popularity. The same "winding-up" dilemma also applies to other galaxies. For the last few decades the favoured attempt to resolve the puzzle has been a complex theory called "density waves." The theory has conceptual problems, has to be arbitrarily and very finely tuned, and has been called into serious question by the Hubble Space Telescope's discovery of very detailed spiral structure in the central hub of the "Whirlpool" galaxy, M51.

According to astronomical observations, galaxies like our own experience about one supernova (a violently-exploding star) every 25 years. The gas and dust remnants from such explosions (like the Crab Nebula above) expand outward rapidly and should remain visible for over a million years. Yet the nearby parts of our galaxy in which we could observe such gas and dust shells contain only about 200 supernova remnants. That number is consistent with only about 7,000 years worth of supernovas.

13. Comets disintegrate too quickly.

According to the evolutionary theory, comets are supposed to be the same age as the solar system, about five billion years. Yet each time a comet orbits close to the sun, it loses so much of its material that it could not survive much longer than about 100,000 years. Many comets have typical ages of less than 10,000 years. Evolutionists explain this discrepancy by assuming that (a) Comets come from an unobserved spherical "Oort cloud" well beyond the orbit of Pluto, (b) Improbable gravitational interactions with infrequently passing stars often knock comets into the solar system, and (c) Other improbable interactions with planets slow down the incoming comets often enough to account for the hundreds of comets observed. So far, none of these assumptions has been substantiated either by observations or realistic calculations. Lately, there has been much talk of the "Kuiper Belt," a disc of supposed comet sources lying in the plane of the solar system just outside the orbit of Pluto. Some asteroid-sized bodies of ice exist in that location, but they do not solve the evolutionists' problem, since according to evolutionary theory, the Kuiper Belt would quickly become exhausted if there were no Oort cloud to supply it.

14. The earth's magnetic field is decaying too fast.

Electrical resistance in the earth's core wears down the electrical cur-rent which produces the earth's magnetic field. That causes the field to lose energy rapidly.

The total energy stored in the earth's magnetic field ("dipole" and "non-dipole") is decreasing with a half-life of 1,465 (+/-165) years. Evolutionary theories explaining this rapid decrease, as well as how the earth could have maintained its magnetic field for billions of years are very complex and inadequate. A much better creationist theory exists. It is straightforward, based on sound physics, and explains many features of the field: its creation, rapid reversals during the Genesis flood, surface intensity decreases and increases until the time of Christ, and a steady decay since then. This theory matches paleomagnetic, historic, and present data, most startlingly with evidence for rapid changes. The main result is that the field's total energy (not surface intensity) has always decayed at least as fast as now. At that rate the field could not be more than 20,000 years old.

THE VIEWS OF
BISHOP JAMES USSHER

Bishop James Ussher (opposite), 1581-1656, was a prolific scholar, famously known as the 'primate of all Ireland' who published a chronology which purposed a biblical creation date of 4004-BC, and still the accepted figure amongst some of today's staunch biblical deity. Uplifted by many, and re-written by subsequent 17th Century authors to fit within this biblical framework. Descartes' of "I think therefore I am" fame is one of them. Ussher's careful calculations of dates, which sounds somewhat beyond daft, but possibly more in keeping then the mathematics behind science, go all the way back to Creation, in the margins of their family Bibles. (In fact, until the 1970s, the Bibles placed in nearly every hotel room by the Gideon Society carried his chronology.) The King James Version of the Bible contains Ussher's famous chronology.

The chronology first appeared in 'The Annals of the Old Testament' a monumental work first published in London in the summer of 1650. In 1654, Ussher added a part two which took his history through Rome's destruction of the Temple in Jerusalem in 70 A.D. The project, which produced 2,000 pages in Latin, occupied twenty years of Ussher's life, (*I know how he feels*). Ussher lived through momentous times, having been born during the reign of Elizabeth and dying, in 1656, under Cromwell. He was a talented fast-track scholar who entered Trinity College in Dublin at the early age of thirteen, became an ordained priest by the age of twenty, and a professor at Trinity by twenty-seven. In 1625, Ussher became the head of the Anglo-Irish Church in Ireland.

As a Protestant bishop in a Catholic land, Ussher's obsession with providing an accurate Biblical history stemmed from a desire to establish the superiority of the scholarship practiced by the clergy of his reformed faith over that of the Jesuits, the resolutely intellectual Roman Catholic order. (Ussher, apparently, had absolutely nothing good to say about "papists" and their "superstitious" faith and "erroneous" doctrine.) Ussher committed himself to establishing a date for Creation that could withstand any challenge. He located and studied thousands of ancient books and manuscripts, written in many different languages. By the time of his death, he had amassed a library of over 10,000 volumes.

The date, forever tied to Bishop Ussher, appears in the first paragraph of the first page of The Annals. Ussher wrote: 'In the beginning, God created heaven and earth which, (according to this chronology) occurred at the beginning of the night which proceeded the 23rd of October in the year 710 of the Julian period.. In the right margin of the page, Ussher computes the date in "Christian" time as 4004 B.C.

Although Ussher brought stunning precision to his chro-nology, Christians for centuries had assumed a history roughly corresponding to his. The Bible itself provides all the informa-tion necessary to conclude that Creation occurred less than 5,000 years before the birth of Christ. Shakespeare, in As You Like It, has his character Rosalind say, "The poor world is al-most six thousand years old." Martin Luther, the great re-former, favoured (liking the round number) 4000 B.C. as a date for creation. Astronomer Johannes Kepler concluded that 3992 B.C. was the probable date.

As palaeontologist Stephen Jay Gould points out in an essay on Ussher, the bishop's calculation of the date of Creation fuelled much ridicule from scientists who pointed to him as "a symbol of ancient and benighted authoritarianism." Few geology textbook writers resisted taking a satirical swing at Ussher in their introductions. How foolish, the authors suggested, to believe that the earth's geologic and fossil history could be crammed into 6,000 years. Gould, while not defending the bishop's chronology, notes that judged by the research traditions and assumptions of his time, Ussher deserves not criticism, but praise for his meticulousness. The questionable premise underlying Ussher's work, of course, is that the Bible is inerrant.

Ussher began his calculation by adding the ages of the twenty-one generations of people of the Hebrew-derived Old Testament, beginning with Adam and Eve. If the Bible is to be believed, they were an exceptionally long-lived lot. Genesis, for example, tells us that "Adam lived 930 years and he died." Adam's great-great-great-great-great-grandson, Methuselah, claimed the longevity record, coming in at 969 years.

Healthier living conditions contributed, or so it was believed, to the long life spans of the early generations of the Bi-ble. Josephus, a Jewish theologian writing in the first century, explained it this way: "Their food was fitter for the prolonga-tion of life...and besides, God afforded them a longer lifespan on account of their virtue."

To calculate the length of time since Creation, knowledge of more than the ages of death of the twenty-one generations was required; one also needed to know the ages of people of each generation at the time the next generation began. Fortu-nately, the Bible provided that information as well. For exam-ple, Genesis says that at the time Adam gave birth to his first son, Seth, he had "lived 130 years." Augustine (as might a lot of people) wondered how a 130-year-old man could sire a child. He concluded that "the earth then produced mightier men" and that they reached puberty much later than did peo-ple of his own generation.

The Old Testament's genealogy took Ussher up to the first destruction of the Temple in Jerusalem during the reign of Persian king Nebuchadnezzar. Ussher's key to precisely dating Creation came from pinning down, by references in non-Christian sources, the precise dates of Nebuchadnezzar's reign. He finally found the answer in a list of Babylonian kings produced by the Greek astronomer Ptolemy in the second cen-tury.

By connecting Greek events to Roman history, Ussher tied the date of Nebuchadnezzar's death (562 B.C.) to the mod-ern Julian calendar. Once the date of 562 B.C. was calculated, there remained only the simple matter of adding 562 years to the 3,442 years represented by the generations of the Old Tes-tament up to that time: 4004.

Ussher next turned his attention to identifying the precise date of Creation. Like many of his contemporary scholars, he assumed that God would choose to create the world on a date that corresponded with the sun being at one of its four cardinal points - either the winter or summer solstice or the vernal or autumnal equinox. This view sprang from the belief that God had a special interest in mathematical and astro-nomical harmony. The deciding factor for Ussher came from Genesis. When Adam and Eve found themselves in the Garden of Eden, the fruit was invitingly ripe.

Ussher reasoned, therefore, that it must have been harvest time, which corresponded with the autumnal equinox: "I have observed that the Sunday, which in the year [4004 B.C.] aforesaid, came nearest the Autumnal Equinox, by Astronomical Tables, happened upon the 23 day of the Julian October."

A London bookseller, Thomas Guy, in 1675 began print-ing Bibles with Ussher's dates printed in the margin of the work. Guy's Bible's became very popular, though their success might be as much attributed to the engravings of bare-breasted biblical women as to the inclusion of Ussher's chronology. In 1701, the Church of England adopted Ussher's dates for use in its official Bible. For the next two centuries, Ussher's dates so commonly appeared in Bibles that his dates "practically ac-quired the authority of the word of God."

Today, there remains a split in the evangelical community between those whose literalist views compel them to accept Bishop Ussher's chronology, or something close to it, ("the young earth creationists") and those who accept fossil evidence and a more metaphorical interpretation of the "days" of Genesis, but who still insist that species were intelligently designed by God, and were not the products of evolution. The date of creation clearly does matter. If Bishop Ussher figured correctly, and every living thing has appeared in only 6,000 years, there simply would have been no time for new species to evolve.

EVOLUTION FROM
A SCIENCE PERSPECTIVE

Before the discovery of radioactivity, James Hutton, (1726-1797) Charles Lyell (1797-1875) and indeed Charles Darwin (1809-1882) were making observations about physical processes acting on rocks. They suggested that in order for processes like evolution and deposition of kilometres of sediment required vast amounts of time; therefore, Earth must be significantly older than human history. Using sedimentation rates and heat flow estimates many scientists attempted to calculate the age of Earth.

Observations of erosion and depositional rates today are slow enough to indicate that a vast amount of time is required to deposit and erode, say, the sedimentary rocks of the Grand Canyon in Arizona. Because there is little physical evidence that physical processes in the past were acting at significantly faster rates, we can conclude that the Earth must have been around for a significant amount of time. Even though these scientists made important observations about the processes acting on the earth, their estimates for the age of the Earth were off by orders of magnitude. In 1862 it was said to be 20 million years old, in 1897 it doubled to 40 million. Two years later it was said to be 90 million years old. In 1947 it was decided to be 3.35 billion years old and in 1956 that was raised to 4.5 billion, now it stands at nearly 5 billion, an excellent time period for evolution to take place.

Darwin's theory of Evolution was influenced by a seemingly old planet

Even in the late 19th century, plate tectonics and radioactivity had not been discovered. Hutton and Lyell had to rely only on visual observations of rocks that formed on the continents ... But what if the earth is only thousands of years old rather than billions then the evolutionary process could not have taken place. Nothing of evolutionary significance could happen in so short a time. For the evolutionist this is an important issue, to him 100,000 years is but a drop in the ocean.

Human evolution, or Anthropogenesis, is the part of biological evolution concerning the emergence of Homo Sapien as a distinct species from other hominans, great apes and placental mammals. It is the subject of a broad scientific inquiry that seeks to understand and describe how this change occurred. The study of human evolution encompasses many scientific disciplines, most notably physical anthropology, linguistics and genetics.

The term "human", in the context of human evolution, refers to the genus Homo, but studies of human evolution usually include other hominins, such as the australopithecines. They say Homo genus diverged from the australopithecines supposedly about 2 million years ago in.

Several typological species of Homo, now extinct, evolved. These include Homo erectus, which inhabited Asia, and Homo neandertharnsis, which inhabited Europe, the downturn is plain to see.

Archaic Homo sapiens is said to have evolved between 400,000 and 250,000 years ago, these figures are recorded from geology (and geology is flawed). The dominant view among scientists is the recent African origin of modern humans that Homo Sapiens evolved in Africa and spread across the globe, replacing populations of Homo Erectus and Homo Neanderthalensis.

Scientists supporting the alternative hypothesis on the multiregional origin of modern humans view modern humans as having evolved as a single, widespread population from existing Homo species, particularly Homo Erectus. The fossil evidence is insufficient to resolve this vigorous debate.

Starting with Homo habilis, humans began using stone tools of increasing sophistication. About 50,000 years ago, human technology and culture began to change more rapidly.

Paleoanthropology is the study of ancient humans based on fossil evidence, tools, and other signs of human habitation. The modern field of paleoanthropology began with the discovery of a Neanderthal skeleton in 1856, although there had been finds elsewhere since 1830.

By 1859, the morphological similarity of humans to certain great apes had been discussed and argued for some time, but the idea of the biological evolution of species in general was not legitimized until Charles Darwin published the Origin of Species in November of that year. Darwin's first book on evolution did not address the specific question of human evolution: "Light will be thrown on the origin of man and his history", was all Darwin wrote on the subject. Nevertheless, the implications of evolutionary theory were clear to contemporary readers as going 'forward' rather than 'backwards'. Debates between Thomas Huxley and Richard Owen focused on human evolution. Huxley convincingly illustrated many of the similarities and differences between humans and apes in his 1863 book 'Evidence as to Man's Place in Nature'. By the time Darwin published his own book on the subject, The Descent of Man, it was already a well-known interpretation of his theory, and the interpretation which made the theory highly controversial.

Even many of Darwin's original supporters such as Alfred Russel Wallace and Charles Lyell did not like the idea that human beings could have evolved their impressive mental capacities and moral sensibilities through natural selection. Since the time of Carolus Linnaeus (1707–1778) who laid the foundations for the modern scheme of Binomial nomenclature, known as the father of modern taxonomy, and is also considered one of the fathers of modern ecology, scientists have considered the great apes to be the closest relatives of human beings because they look very similar.

In the 19th century, they speculated that the closest living relatives of humans are chimpanzees. Based on the natural range of these creatures, they surmised that humans share a common ancestor with other African great apes and that fossils of these ancestors would be found in Africa. It is now accepted by virtually all biologists that humans are not only similar to the great apes but, in fact, are great apes. (Whereas from RT's point of view, it is the other way around).

It was only in the 1920s that such fossils were discovered in Africa. In 1925, Raymond Dart described

Australopithecus africanus. The type specimen was the Taung Child, an australopithecine infant discovered in a cave. The child's remains were a remarkably well-preserved tiny skull and an endocranial cast of the individual's brain. Although the brain was small (410 cm), its shape was rounded, unlike that of chimpanzees and gorillas, and more like a modern human brain. Also, the specimen showed short canine teeth, and the position of the formen magnum was evidence of bipedal locomotion. All of these traits convinced Dart that the Taung baby was a bipedal human ancestor, a transitional form between apes and humans.

Another 20 years would pass before Dart's claims were taken seriously, following the discovery of more fossils that resembled his find. The prevailing view of the time was that a large brain evolved before bipedality. It was thought that intelligence on par with modern humans was a prerequisite to bipedalism. Standing on two feet.

The evolutionary history of the primates can be traced back for some 85 million years (RT would say that would be more like 85 thousand years) as one of the oldest of all surviving placental mammal groups. Most paleontologists consider that primates share a common ancestor with the bats, another extremely ancient lineage, and that this ancestor probably lived during the late Cretaceous, together with the last dinosaurs.

There are now two main schools of thought about the factors that drove human evolution. One theory, the Savannah Theory, first propounded by Raymond Dart, says that the arboreal existence was replaced by a move to the savannah for hunting animals. Another theory, which is still strongly disputed by many researchers, is the Aquatic Ape Hypothesis (AAH). This asserts that wading, swimming and diving for food exerted a strong evolutionary effect on the ancestors of the genus Homo and is in part responsible for the split between the common ancestors of humans and other great apes.

The AAH attempts to explain the large number of physical differences between humans and other apes, such as lack of body hair, larger brains and upright posture, in terms of the methods of feeding and the types of food utilized by early hominids living in coastal and river regions. Though no fossil evidence of an aquatic ape has been found, certain physical differences between humans and other apes seem to support the theory, such as the human's subcutaneous layer of fat, webbing between the fingers and toes, vernix caseosa, and hair growth that follows the direction of water flowing over the body. Based on archaeological and paleontological evidence, it has been possible to infer the ancient dietary practices of various Homo species and to study the role of diet in human (Homo) physical and behavioral evolution.

They say Homo hablis lived from about 2.4 to 1.4 million years ago (mya). Homo habilis, the first species of the genus Homo, evolved in South and East Africa in the late Pliocene or early Pleistocene, 2.5 – 2 mya, when it diverged from the Australopithecines. Homo habilis had smaller molars and larger brains than the Australopithecines, and made tools from stone and perhaps animal bones.

One of the first known hominids, it was nicknamed 'handy man' by its discoverer, Louis Leakey due to its association with stone tools. Some scientists have proposed moving this species out of Homo and into Australopithecus due to its postcranial morphology being more adapted to an arboreal existence rather than to the bipedalism of homo sapiens.

The first fossils of Homo erectus were discovered by Dutch physician Eugene Dubois in 1891 on the Indonesian island of Java. He originally gave the material the name Pithecanthropus erectus based on its morphology that he considered to be intermediate between that of humans and apes. Homo erectus lived from about 1.8 mya to 70,000 years ago. Often the early phase, from 1.8 to 1.25 mya, is considered to be a separate species, Homo ergaster, or it is seen as a subspecies of Homo erectus, Homo erectus ergaster.

In the Early Pleistocene, 1.5 – 1 mya, in Africa, Asia, and Europe, presumably, some populations of Homo habilis evolved larger brains and made more elaborate stone tools; these differences and others are sufficient for anthropologists to classify them as a new species, homo erectus. In addition homo erectus was the first human ancestor to walk truly upright. This was made possible by the evolution of locking knees and a different location of the foramen magnum (the hole in the skull where the spine enters). They may have used fire to cook their meat.

A famous example of homo erectus is Peking Man; others

were found in Asia (notably in Indonesia), Africa, and Europe. Many paleoanthropologists are now using the term homo ergaster for the non-Asian forms of this group, and reserving homo erectus only for those fossils found in the Asian region and meeting certain skeletal and dental requirements which differ slightly from homo ergaster.

Neanderthals are either classified as a sub-species of humans (Homo sapiens neanderthalensis) or as a separate species (Homo neanderthalensis), they lived from about 250,000 to as recent as 30,000 years ago. Also proposed as Homo sapiens neanderthalensis: there is ongoing debate over whether the 'Neanderthal Man' was a separate species, Homo neanderthalensis, or a subspecies of Homo sapiens

Homo Sapien ("sapien" means wise or intelligent) has lived from about 250,000 years ago to the present. Between 400,000 years ago and the second interglacial period in the Middle Pleistocene, around 250,000 years ago, the trend in cranial expansion and the elaboration of stone tool technologies developed, providing evidence for a transition from homo erectus to homo sapiens. The direct evidence suggests there was a migration of homo erectus out of Africa, then a further speciation of homo sapiens from homo erectus in Africa (there is little evidence that this speciation occurred elsewhere). Then a subsequent migration within and out of Africa eventually replaced the earlier dispersed homo erectus. This migration and origin theory is usually referred to as the single-origin theory. However, the current evidence does not preclude multiregional speciation, either. This is a hotly debated area in paleoanthropology.

Current research has established that human beings are genetically highly homogenous, that is the DNA of individuals is more alike than usual for most species, which may have resulted from their relatively recent evolution or the Toba catastrophe. Distinctive genetic characteristics have arisen, however, primarily as the result of small groups of people moving into new environmental circumstances.

Virtually all physical anthropologists agree that homo sapiens evolved out of homo erectus but anthropologists have been divided as to whether homo sapiens evolved as one interconnected species from homo erectus. According to the Out of Africa Model, developed by Chris Stringer and Peter Andrews, modern homo sapiens evolved in Africa 200,000 years ago. Homo sapiens began migrating from Africa between 70,000 – 50,000 years ago and would eventually replace existing hominid species in Europe and Asia. The Out of Africa Model has gained support by recent research using mitochondrial DNA (mtDNA). After analysing genealogy trees constructed using 133 types of mtDNA, they concluded that all were descended from a woman from Africa, dubbed Mitochondrial Eve.

In the western world the modern scientific concept was developed by Scottish geologist James Hutton famous for his work on unconformities, where horizontal and near vertical rock lay alongside each other. The pioneering fieldwork during the Scottish Enlightenment provided evidence that the Earth is far older than generally believed. It was Hutton that led the way in influencing Charles Darwin and the theory of evolution.

Science in succeeding centuries has established the age of the Earth as between four and five billion years, with an exceedingly long history of change and development but this is based on geology, (but geology is flawed).

An understanding of geologic history and the concomitant history of life requires a comprehension of time which at first was rather disconcerting. As mathematician John Playfair, one of Hutton's friends and colleagues in the Scottish Enlightenment, later remarked upon seeing the strata of the angular unconformity at Siccar Point with Hutton and James Hall in June 1788, "the mind seemed to grow giddy by looking so far into the abyss of time."

Hutton's words, "we find no vestige of a beginning, no prospect of an end," which was in stark contrast to the prevailing Genesis creation story, which held that the Earth has existed for only a few thousand years. It was still hazardous in Hutton's time to oppose the young Earth creationism doctrine which was then dominant.

Proponents of scientific theories which contradicted scriptural interpretations could not only lose their academic appointments but were legally answerable to charges of heresy or blasphemy, charges which, even as late as the 18th century (1700s) in Great Britain, sometimes resulted in a death sentence.

Hutton's comprehension of deep time as a crucial scientific concept was developed further by Charles Lyell in his "Principles of Geology" (1830). Naturalist and evolutionary theorist Charles Darwin studied Lyell's book exhaustively during his expedition on the HMS Beagle in the 1830s.

Charles Lyell's first book, Principle of Geology, was also his most famous, most influential, and most important. First published in three volumes in 1830-33, it established Lyell's credentials as an important geological theorist and propounded the doctrine of uniformitarianism. It was a work of synthesis, backed by his own personal observations on his travels. The central argument in his book was that "the present is the key to the past" ... whereas RT would say "The Past is the key to the Furture".

Geological remains from the distant past can, and should, be explained by reference to geological processes now in operation and thus directly observable. Lyell's interpretation of geologic change as the steady accumulation of minute changes over enormously long spans of time was a powerful influence on the young Charles Darwin.

Lyell asked the captain of HMS Beagle, Robert FitzRoy, to search for erratic boulders on the survey voyage of the Beagle, and just before it set out FitzRoy gave Darwin Volume 1 of the first edition of Lyell's Principles. When the Beagle made its first stop ashore at St Jago Darwin found rock formations which seen "through Lyell's eyes" gave him a revolutionary insight into the geological history of the island, an insight he applied throughout his travels.

Hutton's ideas on geology were clarified in Charles

Lyell's books, which Charles Darwin read with enthusiasm during his voyage on the Beagle, and it remained to Darwin independently to develop the idea of natural selection to explain The Origin of Species and bring it to the forefront of public consciousness at the same time as providing the voluminous evidence necessary to win over the scientific community to the theory.

Hutton proposed a steady-state theory whereby the only processes occurring through time are those that we can see now. He suggested that while the Earth had a beginning we could not see it, as all traces had been obliterated by subsequent cycles of *"erosion and re-deposition"*.

"No vestige of a beginning, no prospect of an end" was how he put it.

And I repeat ... Geology forms the foundations of all our scientific beliefs and principles, therefore if a theory at the very grass roots of geology is wrong, it would cause a chain reaction throughout all knowledge, changing the way we understand and perceive things. By simple re-looking at this one geological fact of life correctly, ie, beach pebbles, a picture will unfold that will enable you to see the most exquisite pattern to the workings of nature. A pattern that can only make you think the world we live in has all the markings of being programmed by some higher authority that exists somewhere beyond our comprehension.

Unlock the pebble phenomenon (the missing link) and not only will it confirm that the age of the planet has been severely miscalculated, but it will bring to light geological and scientific misjudgments on an unprecedented scale. Thus leaving the door wide open for the supernatural side of life to shine through, and my goodness shine through it does! To better understand what lies beyond consciousness and to familiarize yourself with the afterlife you will need to convince yourself that pebbles are formed by the principle of tidemark rather than the principle of erosion.

If this pebble phenomenon is right it would solve many of the great riddles that have been previously left unanswered. If you can understand 'sand to pebble' rather than pebbles to sand, then we can knock a few noughts off our understanding of deep-time, for instance using the old principle of pebbles to sand, our mathematical figures show the KT boundary happened 65 million year ago, however, using our new principle, sand to pebble, we could, as a ball-park figure, say it happened 65 thousand years ago.

So we have two stories – Pebbles to Sand' and Sand to Pebbles' one tells one story whilst the other tells another. Pebbles' forming by the principle of tidemark is one and Pebbles' forming by the principle of erosion is the other.

One we live by today which set the foundations for an old planet, and the other, which is about to set the foundation for a young planet. Which one would you prefer; the ideology of an old planet or the ideology of a young planet … the choice is yours?

Everyone's opinion is valid, we all have a voice and we all deserve to have our say, it is my opinion that we should all look at the world around us, and form our own philosophies through personal reasoning and contemplation. Free thinking will always be the road to discovery, and by looking at the world with fresh eyes you may discover extraordinary things, and one day in the future you may agree that the pebbles on the beach do indeed get bigger.

RADIOMETRIC DATING

A large advance in geology in the advent of the 20th century was the ability to use ratios of radioactive isotopes to find the amount of 'time' that has passed since a rock passed through a particular temperature.

Radiometric dating, often called radioactive dating, came in 1905 and the currently accepted age of the Earth was ascertained using that method. It is a technique used to date materials, usually based on a comparison between the observed abundance of a naturally occurring radioactive isotope and its decay products, using known decay rates. It is the principal source of information about the absolute age of rocks and other geological features, including the age of the earth itself, and can be used to date a wide range of natural and man-made materials.

Among the best-known techniques are radiocarbon dating, potassium-argon dating and uranium-lead dating. By allowing the establishment of geological timescales, it provides a significant source of information about the ages of fossils and the deduced rates of evolutionary change. Radiometric dating is also used to date archaeological materials, including ancient artifacts.

Different methods of radiometric dating vary in the timescale over which they are accurate and the materials to which they can be applied.

All ordinary matter is made up of combinations of

chemical elements, each with its own atomic number, indicating the number of protons in the atomatic nucleus. Additionally, elements may exist in different isotopes, with each isotope of an element differing in the number of neutrons in the nucleus.

A particular isotope of a particular element is called a nuclide. Some nuclides are inherently unstable. That is, at some point in time, an atom of such a nuclide will spontaneously transform into a different nuclide. This transformation may be accomplished in a number of different ways, including radioactive decay, either by emission of particles (usually electrons (beta decay) positrons or alpha particals) or by spontaneous fission, and electron capture.

While the moment in time at which a particular nucleus decays is unpredictable, a collection of atoms of a radioactive nuclide decays exponentially at a rate described by a parameter known as the half-life, usually given in units of years when discussing dating techniques. After one half-life has elapsed, one half of the atoms of the nuclide in question will have decayed into a "daughter" nuclide or decay product.

In many cases, the daughter nuclide itself is radioactive, resulting in a decay chain, eventually ending with the formation of a stable (nonradioactive) daughter nuclide; each step in such a chain is characterized by a distinct half-life. In these cases, usually the half-life of interest in radiometric dating is the longest one in the chain, which is the rate-limiting factor in the ultimate transformation of the radioactive nuclide into its stable daughter. Isotopic systems that have been exploited for radiometric dating have half-lives ranging from only about 10 years to over 100 billion years (ie, tritium and samarium-147).

In general, the half-life of a nuclide depends solely on its nuclear properties; it is not affected by external factors such as temperture, pressure, chemical environment, or presence of a magnetic or electric field. (For some nuclides which decay by the process of electron capture, such as Beryllium-7, Strontium-85, and Zirconium-89, the decay rate may be slightly affected by local electron density, therefore these isotopes may not be as suitable for radiometric dating.) But in general, the half-life of any nuclide is essentially a constant.

Therefore, in any material containing a radioactive nuclide, the proportion of the original nuclide to its decay product(s) changes in a predictable way as the original nuclide decays over time. This predictability allows the relative abundances of related nuclides to be used as a clock that measures the time from the incorporation of the original nuclide(s) into a material to the present.

The processes that form specific materials are often conveniently selective as to what elements they incorporate during their formation. In the simplest case, the material will incorporate a parent nuclide and reject the daughter nuclide. In this case, the only atoms of the daughter nuclide present in a sample must have been deposited by radioactive decay since the sample formed.

When a material incorporates both the parent and

daughter nuclides at the time of formation, a correction must be made for the initial proportion of the radioactive substance and its daughter; generally this is done by construction of an isochron, e.g. in rabidium-strontium dating.

Accurate radiometric dating generally requires that neither the parent nuclide nor the daughter product can enter or leave the material after its formation, that the parent has a long enough half-life that it will still be present in significant amounts at the time of measurement (except as described below under "Dating with shortlived extinct radionuclides"), the half-life of the parent is accurately known, and enough of the daughter product is produced to be accurately measured and distinguished from the initial amount of the daughter present in the material.

The procedures used to isolate and analyze the parent and daughter nuclides must be precise and accurate. This normally involves isotope ratio mass spectrometry. If a material that selectively rejects the daughter nuclide is heated, any daughter nuclides that have been accumulated over time will be lost through diffusion, setting the isotopic "clock" to zero. The temperature at which this happens is known as the blocking temperture or closure temperature and is specific to a particular material and isotopic system. These temperatures are experimentally determined in the lab by artificially resetting sample minerals using a high-temperature furnace.

Considering that radioactive parent elements decay to stable daughter elements, the mathematical expression that relates radioactive decay to geologic time, called the age equation.

$$t = \frac{1}{\lambda}\ln\left(1 + \frac{D}{P}\right)$$

Where:

t = age of the sample
D = number of atoms of the daughter isotope in the sample
P = number of atoms of the parent isotope in the sample
λ = decay constant of the parent isotope
ln = natural logarithm

The decay constant (or rate of decay) is the fraction of a number of atoms of a radioactive nuclide that disintegrates in a unit of time. The decay constant is inversely proportional to the radioactive half-life of the parent isotope, which can be obtained from tables such as the one on this page.

The trouble is 'The Age of the Sample Material' has been mis-calculated and makes our mathematical sums fundmentally flawed.

Although radiometric dating is accurate in principle, the precision is very dependent on the care with which the procedure is performed. The possible confounding effects of initial contamination of parent and daughter isotopes have to be considered, as do the effects of any loss or gain of such isotopes since the sample was created.

Precision is enhanced if measurements are taken on different samples from the same rock body but at different locations. Alternatively, if several different minerals can be dated from the same sample and are assumed to be formed by the same event and were in equilibrium with the reservoir when they formed, they should form an isochron. Finally, correlation between different isotopic dating methods may be required to confirm the age of a sample.

The precision of a dating method depends in part on the half-life of the radioactive isotope involved. For instance, carbon-14 has a half-life of about 6000 years. After an organism has been dead for 60,000 years, so little carbon-14 is left in it that accurate dating becomes impossible. On the other hand, the concentration of carbon-14 falls off so steeply that the age of relatively young remains can be determined precisely to within a few decades. The isotope used in uranium – thorium dating has a longer half-life, but other factors make it more accurate than radiocarbon dating.

Radiometric dating can be performed on samples as small as a billionth of a gram using a mass spectrometer. The mass spectrometer was invented in the 1940s and began to be used in radiometric dating in the 1950s. The mass spectrometer operates by generating a beam of ionized atoms from the sample under test. The ions then travel through a magnetic field, which diverts them into different sampling sensors, known as 'Faraday cups', depending on their mass and level of ionization. On impact in the cups, the ions set up a very weak current that can be measured to determine the rate of impacts and the relative concentrations of different atoms in the beams.

The uranium-lead radiometric dating scheme is one of the oldest available, as well as one of the most highly respected. It has been refined to the point that the error in dates of rocks about three billion years old is no more than two million years.

Uranium-lead dating is often performed on the mineral zircon ($ZrSiO4$), though it can be used on other materials. Zircon incorporates uranium atoms into its crystalline structure as substitutes for zirconium, but strongly rejects lead. It has a very high blocking temperature, is resistant to mechanical weathering and is very chemically inert. Zircon also forms multiple crystal layers during metamorphic events, which each may record an isotopic age of the event. In situ micro-beam analysis can be achieved via laser ICP-MS or SIMS techniques.

One of its great advantages is that any sample provides two clocks, one based on uranium-235's decay to lead-207 with a half-life of about 700 million years, and one based on uranium-238's decay to lead-206 with a half-life of about 4.5 billion years, providing a built-in crosscheck that allows accurate determination of the age of the sample even if some of the lead has been lost.

Two other radiometric techniques are used for long-term dating. Potassium-argon dating involves electron capture or positron decay of potassium-40 to argon-40. Potassium-40 has a half-life of 1.3 billion years, and so this method is applicable to the oldest rocks. Radioactive potassium-40 is common in micas, feldspars, and hornblends, though the blocking temperature is fairly low in these materials, about 125°C (mica) to 450°C (hornblende).

Rubidium-strontium dating is based on the beta decay of rubidium -87 to strontium -87, with a half-life of 50 billion years. This scheme is used to date old igneous and metamorphic rocks, and has also been used to date lunar samples. Blocking temperatures are so high that they are not a concern. Rubidium-strontium dating is not as precise as the uranium-lead method, with errors of 30 to 50 million years for a 3-billion-year-old sample.

Carbon-14 however, is a radioactive isotope of carbon, with a half-life of 5,730 years (very short compared with the above). In other radiometric dating methods, the heavy parent isotopes were synthesized in the explosions of massive stars that scattered materials through the Galaxy, to be formed into planets and other stars. The parent isotopes have been decaying since that time, and so any parent isotope with a short half-life should be extinct by now.

Carbon-14 is an exception. It is continuously created through collisions of neutrons generated by cosmic rays with nitrogen in the upper atmosphere. The carbon-14 ends up as a trace component in atmospheric carbon dioxide (CO_2).

An organism acquires carbon from carbon dioxide during its lifetime. Plants acquire it through photosynthesis, and animals acquire it from consumption of plants and other animals. When an organism dies, it ceases to intake new carbon-14 and the existing isotope decays with a characteristic half-life (5730 years). The proportion of carbon-14 left when the remains of the organism are examined provides an indication of the time lapsed since its death. The carbon-14 dating limit lies around 58,000 to 62,000 years.

The rate of creation of carbon-14 appears to be roughly constant, as cross-checks of carbon-14 dating with other dating methods show it gives consistent results. However, local eruptions of volcanoes or other events that give off large amounts of carbon dioxide can reduce local concentrations of carbon-14 and give inaccurate dates. The releases of carbon dioxide into the biosphere as a consequence of industrialization have also depressed the proportion of carbon-14 by a few percent; conversely, the amount of carbon-14 was increased by above-ground nuclear bomb tests that were conducted into the early 1960s.

Also, an increase in the solar wind or the earth's magnetic field above the current value would depress the amount of carbon-14 created in the atmosphere. These effects are corrected for by the calibration of the radiocarbon dating scale. Another relatively short-range dating technique is based on the decay of uranium-238 into thorium-230, a substance with a half-life of about 80,000 years. It is accompanied by a sister process, in which uranium-235 decays into protactinium-231, which has a half-life of 34,300 years.

While uranium is water-soluble, thorium and protactinium are not, and so they are selectively precipitated into ocean-floor sediments, from which their ratios are measured. The scheme has a range of several hundred thousand years.

Natural sources of radiation in the environment knock loose electrons in, say, a piece of pottery, and these electrons accumulate in defects in the material's crystal lattice structure. Heating the object will release the captured electrons, producing a luminescence. When the sample is heated, at a certain temperature it will glow from the emission of electrons released from the defects, and this glow can be used to estimate the age of the sample to a threshold of approximately 15 percent of its true age.

The date of a rock is reset when volcanic activity remelts it. The date of a piece of pottery is reset by the heat of the kiln. Typically temperatures greater than 400 degrees Celsius will reset the 'clock'. This is termed thermoluminescence.

Finally, fission track dating involves inspection of a polished slice of a material to determine the density of "track" markings left in it by the spontaneous fission of uranium-238 impurities.

The uranium content of the sample has to be known, but that can be determined by placing a plastic film over the polished slice of the material, and bombarding it with slow neutrons. This causes induced fission of uranium 235 impurities, 235U, as opposed to the spontaneous fission of 238U. The fission tracks produced by this process are recorded in the plastic film. The uranium content of the material can then be calculated from the number of tracks and the neutron flux.

This scheme has application over a wide range of geologic dates. For dates up to a few million years micas, tektites (glass fragments from volcanic eruptions), and meteorites are best used. Older materials can be dated using zircon, apatite, titanite, epidote and garnet which have a variable amount of uranium content. Because the fission tracks are healed by temperatures over about 200°C the technique has limitations as well as benefits. The technique has potential applications for detailing the thermal history of a deposit.

Large amounts were produced by irradiation of seawater during atmospheric detonations of nuclear weapons between 1952 and 1958. The residence time of isotope chlorine in the atmosphere is about 1 week. Thus, as an event marker of 1950s water in soil and ground water, is also useful for dating waters less than 50 years before the present. 36Cl has seen use in other areas of the geological sciences, including dating ice and sediments.

At the beginning of the solar system there were several relatively shortlived radionuclides present within the solar nebula. These radionuclides, possibly produced by the explosion of a supernova, are extinct today but their decay products can be detected in very old material such as meteorites. Measuring the decay products of extinct radionuclides with a mass spectrometer and using isochronplots it is possible to determine relative ages between different events in the early history of the solar system. Dating methods based on extinct radionuclides can also be calibrated with the U-Pb method to give absolute ages.

THE PUBLISHERS AND AGENTS WHO REJECTED RT

The Society of Authors – September 1992

Bible Society – September 1992

Penguin Books – October 1992

Pan Books – October 1992

Marion Boyars Publishers – October 1992

Jane Judd – October 1992

The society for Promoting Christian Knowledge – October 1992

Bantam Press – October 1992

Peter Halban Publishers – October 1992

IVP – November 1992

Souvenir Press – November 1992

Scripture Press November 1992

Lion publishing November 1992

Harper Collins – November 1992

Lion Publishing – November 1992

Eagle & highland books – November 1992

Element Books – November 1992

St Pauls Publishers – December 1992

Darton Longman & Todd – December 1992

Hodder & Stoughton Publishers – December 1992

The Lutterworth Press – December 1992

T&T Clark – December 1992

John Donald Publishers – December 1992

Eagle – December 1992

The Octagon Press Ltd – December 1992
Scripture Union – January 1993
Harper Collins 'Religious' - January 1993
Darton Longman & Todd – March 1993
University of Greenwich – April 1993
The Book Guild – April 1993
Darton Longman & Todd – April 1993
NewScientist May 1993
David Grossman – May 1993
ABA – June 1993
The Society for Promoting Christian Knowledge – June 1993
Peters Fraser & Dunlop – June 1993
BBC Enterprises – June 1993
Oxford University July 1993
Cambridge University 'faculty board of classics' - July 1993
Cambridge University – August 4th & 13th 1993
"Department of Earth Sciences"
William Morris Agency – October 1993
Reading university – November 1993
Watch Tower December 1993
Mowbray publishing - January 1994
Cambridge University – February 1994
Cambridge University – March 1994
"Department of Earth Sciences"
The Book Guild – April 5th + 30th 1993
Curtis Brown & Farquharson – May 1993
Telegraph Magazine – May 1993
The Observer – May 1993

You Magazine – June 1993
Curtis Brown & Farquharson – July 1993
Transworld – July 1993
4th Estate – April 1994
Bantam Press – May 1994
Souvenir Press – June 1994
Bantam Press – July 1994
Souvenir Press – July 1994
The Book Guild - July, August, September, November 1994
Shepheard-Walwyn Publishers – October 1994
Curtis Brown - November 1994
Hodder Stoughton publishers - November 1994
Jacintha Alexander Associates – November 1994
Aitken, Stone & Wylie – November 1994
Rosica Colin Ltd – December 1994
Rupert Crew Ltd – December 1994
Serafina Clarke – December 1994
Jonathan Clowes Ltd – December 1994
Dianne Coles - December 1994
Blake Friedmann – December 1994
London School of Economics - December 1994
Harriet Cruickshank – December 1994
Jane Conway-Gordon - January 1995
A & B January 1995
Arthur James Book Publishers – February 1995
Bantam Press – March 1995
Harper Collins - April 1995
The Society for Promoting Christian Knowledge – May 1995

Lion publishing – May 1995
Michael Joseph and Pelham books – May 1995
Lion Publishing – May 1995
Bantam Press – May 1995
St Pauls Publishing – June 1995
SCM Press June 1995
Macmillan – June 1995
Penguin – July 1995
Routledge – July 1995
Darton Longman & Todd - August 1995
Bantam Press – September 1995
Bantam & Bantam Press – October 1995
Souvenir Press October 1995
Hutchinson – November 1995
Random House UK – November 1995
Cambridge University Press – December 1995
Gabriel Communication Ltd – December 1995
Element Books – January 1996
Bantam & bantam Press – February 1996
Bantam & Bantam Press – March 1996
Transworld Publishers – April 1996
Laurence Pollinger Ltd – April 1996
Transworld Publishers – April 1996
William Morris Agency – May 1996
Bellew Publishing Company May 1996
Peters Fraser & Dunlop – May 1996
Athlone – May 1996
Dartmouth Publishing Company – May 1996

Academy Editions – May 1996

Michael Joseph – June 1996

Cambridge University Press – June 1996

Search Press Ltd – June 1996

Aurum Press – June 1996

Cassell – July 1996

Kingsway Publications – May 1996

Cambridge University Press – June 1996

The Lutterworth Press – July 1996

David Bolt Associates – July 1996

Constable Publishers – August 1996

David Bolt – October 1996

Catholic Truth Society – January 1997

Cassell – February 1997

Transworld Publishers – February 1997

Gateway Books – February 1997

Souvenir Press – April 1997

Cambridge University Press – April 1997

Transworld Publishers – May 1997

Harper Collins Publishers May 1997

Macmillan Press – May 1997

Lion Publishing – June 1997

Oneworld Publication – September 1997

National Christian Education Council – September 1997

The Methodist Church – October 1997

Monarch 'Book of Substance' – October 1997

Methodist Publishing – October 1997

The Orion publishing group - November 1997

Paternoster Publishing – November 1997
Transworld – November 1997
Watson Little Ltd Authors Agents – December 1997
David Higham Associates – December 1997
Macmillan General Books – December 1997
Macmillan General Books – January 1998
Oxford University Press - February 1998
Cambridge University Press – February 1998
Virgin Publishing – March 1998
Burns & Oates – March 1998
Element Books – April 1998
The Sunday Times – June 1998
William Morris Agency – July 1998
Christopher Little – October 1998
Chapman & Vincent Literary Agent October 1998
The Sunday Times – October 1998
The Church of England – November 1998
The Mail on Sunday – November 1998
Church Times – November 1998
The Guardian - December 1998
Fortean Times – December 1998
The Times – March 1999
Transworld Publishers – June 1999
Souvenir Press – July 1999
Night & Day - The Mail on Sunday Review – August 1999
Prediction – August 1999
The Philosopher – September 1999
The Guardian – September 1999

Focus Magazine for Writers – October 1999
RPA New Humanist – February 2001
National Radio, Talk Sport, James Whale, – March 2006

REFERENCES FOR THE
YOUNG EARTH ARGUMENT

1. Scheffler, H. and Elsasser, H., Physics of the Galaxy and In-terstellar Matter, Springer-Verlag (1987) Berlin, pp. 352–353, 401–413.

2. D. Zaritsky, H-W. Rix, and M. Rieke, Inner spiral structure of the galaxy M51, Nature 364:313–315 (July 22, 1993).

3. Davies, K., Distribution of supernova remnants in the galaxy, Proceedings of the Third International Conference on Crea-tionism, vol. II, Creation Science Fellowship (1994), Pitts-burgh, PA, pp. 175–184, order from http://www.creationicc.org/.

4. Steidl, P. F., Planets, comets, and asteroids, Design and Ori-gins in Astronomy, pp. 73-106, G. Mulfinger, ed., Creation Re-search Society Books (1983), order from http://www.creationresearch.org/.

5. Whipple, F. L., Background of modern comet theory, Nature 263:15–19 (2 September 1976). Levison, H. F. et al. See also: The mass disruption of Oort Cloud comets, Science 296:2212–2215 (21 June 2002).

6. Milliman, John D. and James P. M. Syvitski, Geomor-phic/tectonic control of sediment discharge to the ocean: the importance of small mountainous rivers, The Journal of Geol-ogy, vol. 100, pp. 525–544 (1992).

7. Hay, W. W., et al., Mass/age distribution and composition of sediments on the ocean floor and the global rate of sediment subduction, Journal of Geophysical Research, 93(B12):14,933–14,940 (10 December 1988).

8. Meybeck, M., Concentrations des eaux fluviales en elements majeurs et apports en solution aux oceans, Revue de Géologie Dynamique et de Géographie Physique 21(3):215 (1979).

9. Sayles, F. L. and P. C. Mangelsdorf, Cation-exchange characteristics of Amazon River suspended sediment and its reaction with seawater, Geochimica et Cosmochimica Acta 43:767–779 (1979).

10. Austin, S. A. and D. R. Humphreys, The sea's missing salt: a dilemma for evolutionists, Proceedings of the Second Interna-tional Conference on Creationism, vol. II, Creation Science Fel-lowship (1991), Pittsburgh, PA, pp. 17–33, order from http://www.creationicc.org/.

11. Nevins, S., [Austin, S. A.], Evolution: the oceans say no!, Impact No. 8 (Nov. 1973) Institute for Creation Research.

12. Humphreys, D. R., The earth's magnetic field is still losing energy, Creation Research Society Quarterly, 39(1):3–13, June 2002.
    http://www.creationresearch.org/crsq/articles/39/39_1/GeoMag.htm.

13. Humphreys, D. R., Reversals of the earth's magnetic field during the Genesis flood, Proceedings of the

First International Conference on Creationism, vol. II, Creation Science Fellow-ship (1986), Pittsburgh, PA, pp. 113–126, out of print but con-tact *http://www.creationicc.org/ for help in locating copies.*

14. Coe, R. S., M. Prévot, and P. Camps, New evidence for extraordinarily rapid change of the geomagnetic field during a reversal, Nature 374:687–92 (20 April 1995).

15. Humphreys, D. R., Physical mechanism for reversals of the earth's magnetic field during the flood, Proceedings of the Second International Conference on Creationism, vol. II, Creation Science Fellowship (1991), Pittsburgh, PA, pp. 129–142, order from *http://www.creationicc.org/.*

16. Austin, S. A. and J. D. Morris, Tight folds and clastic dikes as evidence for rapid deposition and deformation of two very thick stratigraphic sequences, Proceedings of the First Inter-national Conference on Creationism, vol. II, Creation Science Fellowship (1986), Pittsburgh, PA, pp. 3–15, out of print, contact *http://www.creationicc.org/* for help in locating copies.

17. Gibbons A., Calibrating the mitochondrial clock, Science 279:28–29 (2 January 1998).

18. Cherfas, J., Ancient DNA: still busy after death, Science 253:1354–1356 (20 September 1991). Cano, R. J., H. N. Poinar, N. J. Pieniazek, A. Acra, and G. O. Poinar, Jr. Amplification and sequencing of DNA

from a 120-135-million-year-old weevil, Nature 363:536–8 (10 June 1993). Krings, M., A. Stone, R. W. Schmitz, H. Krainitzki, M. Stoneking, and S. Pääbo, Neandertal DNA sequences and the origin of modern humans, Cell 90:19–30 (Jul 11, 1997). Lindahl, T, Unlocking nature's ancient secrets, Nature 413:358–359 (27 September 2001).

19. Vreeland, R. H.,W. D. Rosenzweig, and D. W. Powers, Isolation of a 250 million-year-old halotolerant bacterium from a pri-mary salt crystal, Nature 407:897–900 (19 October 2000).

20. Schweitzer, M., J. L. Wittmeyer, J. R. Horner, and J. K. Toporski, Soft-Tissue vessels and cellular preservation in Tyrannosaurus rex, Science 207:1952–1955 (25 March 2005).

21. Gentry, R. V., Radioactive halos, Annual Review of Nuclear Science 23:347–362 (1973).

22. Gentry, R. V. , W. H. Christie, D. H. Smith, J. F. Emery, S. A. Reynolds, R. Walker, S. S. Christy, and P. A. Gentry, Radiohalos in coalified wood: new evidence relating to time of uranium introduction and coalification, Science 194:315–318 (15 Octo-ber 1976).

23. Gentry, R. V., Radiohalos in a radiochronological and cosmological perspective, Science 184:62–66 (5 April 1974).

24. Snelling, A. A. and M. H. Armitage, Radiohalos—a tale of three granitic plutons, Proceedings of the Fifth International Confer-ence on Creationism, vol. II,

Creation Science Fellowship (2003), Pittsburgh, PA, pp. 243–267, order from http://www.creationicc.org/.

25. Gentry, R. V., G. L. Glish, and E. H. McBay, Differential helium retention in zircons: implications for nuclear waste containment, Geophysical Research Letters 9(10):1129–1130 (Oc-tober 1982).

26. Humphreys, D. R, et al., Helium diffusion age of 6,000 years supports accelerated nuclear decay, Creation Research Society Quarterly 41(1):1–16 (June 2004). See archived article on fol-lowing page of the CRS website: *http://www.creationresearch.org/crsq/articles/41/41_1/Helium.htm.*

27. Baumgardner, J. R., et al., Measurable 14C in fossilized organic materials: confirming the young earth creation-flood model, Proceedings of the Fifth International Conference on Creationism, vol. II, Creation Science Fellowship (2003), Pitts-burgh, PA, pp. 127–142. Archived at *http://globalflood.org/papers/2003ICCc14.html.*

28. McDougall, I., F. H. Brown, and J. G. Fleagle, Stratigraphic placement and age of modern humans from Kibish, Ethiopia, Nature 433(7027):733–736 (17 February 2005).

29. Deevey, E. S., The human population, Scientific American 203:194–204 (September 1960).

30. Marshack, A., Exploring the mind of Ice Age man, National Geographic 147:64–89 (January 1975).

31. Dritt, J. O., Man's earliest beginnings: discrepancies in evolutionary timetables, Proceedings of the Second International Conference on Creationism, vol. II, Creation Science Fellow-ship (1991), Pittsburgh, PA, pp. 73–78, order from http://www.creationicc.org/.

LIST OF DEITIES
OF ANCIENT EGYPT

Aken - Ferryman to the underworld.

Ammit - crocodile-headed devourer in Duat, not a true deity.

Amun (*also spelled Amen*) - the hidden one, a local creator deity later married to Mut after rising in importance.

Amunet - female aspect of the primordial concept of air in the Ogdoad cosmogony; was depicted as a cobra snake or a snake-headed woman.

Anubis (*also spelled Yinepu*) - dog or jackal god of embalming and tomb-caretaker who watches over the dead.

Anuket - goddess of the Nile River, the child of Satis and among the Elephantine triad of deities; temple on the Island of Seheil, giver of life and fertility, gazelle-headed.

Apep (*also spelled Apophis*) - evil serpent of the Underworld, enemy of Ra and formed from a length of Neith's spit during her creation of the world.

Apis - the Apis bull probably was at first a fertility figure concerned with the propagation of grain and herds; but he became associated with Ptah, the paramount deity of the Memphis area and also, with Osiris (as User-Hapi) and Sokaris, later gods of the dead and the underworld. As Apis-Atum he was associated with the solar cult and was often represented with the sun-disk of the cow deity between his horns, being her offspring. The Apis bull often represented a king who became a deity after death, suggesting an earlier ritual in which the king was sacrificed.

The Aten - the sun disk or globe worshipped primarily during the Amarna Period in the eighteenth dynasty when representing a monotheistic deity advanced by Amenhotep IV, who took the name Akhenaten.

Atum - a creator deity, and the setting sun.

Bast - goddess, protector of the pharaoh and a solar deity where the sun could be seen shining in her eyes at night, a lioness, house cat, cat-bodied or cat-headed woman, also known as Bastet when superseded by Sekhmet.

Bat - represented the cosmos and the essence of the soul (Ba), cow goddess who gave authority to the king, cult originated in Hu and persisted widely until absorbed as an aspect of Hathor after the eleventh dynasty; associated with the sistrum and the ankh

Bes - dwarfed demigod - associated with protection of the household, particularly childbirth, and entertainment.

The four sons of Horus - personifications of the containers for the organs of the deceased pharaohs - Imsety in human form, contained the liver and was protected by Isis; Hapi in baboon form, contained the lungs and was protected by Nephthys; Duamutef in jackal form, contained the stomach and was protected by Neith; Qebehsenuef in hawk form, contained the large intestines and was protected by Serket.

Geb - god of the Earth and first ruler of Egypt.

Hapy (*also spelled Hapi*) - god embodied by the Nile, and who represents life and fertility.

Hathor (*also spelled Hethert*) - among the oldest of Egyptian deities - often depicted as the cow, a cow-goddess, sky-goddess and tree-goddess who was the mother to the pharaoh and earlier to the universe, the golden calf of the bible, and later goddess of love and music.

Heget (*also spelled Heqet*) - goddess of childbirth and fertility, who breathed life into humans at birth, represented as a frog or a frog-headed woman.

Horus (*also spelled Heru*) - the falcon-headed god. Includes multiple forms or potentially different gods, including Heru the son of Isis, god of pharaohs and Upper Egypt, and Heru the elder

Isis (*also spelled Aset*) - goddess of magical power and healing, "She of the Throne" who was represented as the throne, also later as the wife of Osiris and as the protector of the dead.

Iusaaset - the great one who comes forth, the goddess who was called the mother and grandmother of all of the deities and later, the "shadow" of Atum or Atum-Ra.

Khepry (*also spelled Khepra*) - the scarab beetle, the embodiment of the dawn.

Khnum - a creator deity, god of the inundation.

Khonsu - the son of Amun and Mut, whose name means "wanderer", which probably refers to the passage of the moon across the sky, as he was a lunar deity. In the late period, he was also considered an important god of healing.

Kuk - the personification of darkness that often took the form of a frog-headed god, whose consort was the snake-headed Kauket.

Maahes - he who is true beside her, a lion prince, son of Bast in Lower Egypt and of Sekhmet in Upper Egypt and sharing their natures, his father varied — being the current chief male deity of the time and region, a god of war, weather, and protector of matrilineality, his cult arrived during the New Kingdom era perhaps from Nubia and was centred in Taremu and Per-Bast, associated with the high priests of Amon, the knife, lotuses, and devouring captives.

Ma'at - a goddess who personified concept of truth, balance, justice, and order - represented as a woman, sitting or standing, holding a sceptre in one hand and an ankh in the other - thought to have created order out of the primal chaos and was responsible for maintaining the order of the universe and all of its inhabitants, to prevent a return to chaos.

Mafdet - she who runs swiftly, early deification of legal justice (execution) as a cheetah, ruling at judgment hall in Duat where enemies of the pharaoh were decapitated with Mafdet's claw; alternately, a cat, a mongoose, or a leopard protecting against vermin, snakes, and scorpions; the bed upon which royal mummies were placed in murals.

Menhit - goddess of war - depicted as a lioness-goddess and therefore becoming associated with Sekhmet.

Meretseger - goddess of the valley of the kings, a cobra-goddess, sometimes triple-headed, dweller on the top of or the personification of the pyramid-shaped mountain, Al-Qurn, which overlooked the tombs of the pharaohs in the Valley of the Kings.

Meskhenet - goddess of childbirth, and the creator of each person's Ka, a part of their soul, thereby associated with fate.

Menthu (*also spelled Montu*) - an ancient god of war - nomad - represented strength, virility, and victory.

Min - represented in many different forms, but was often represented in male human form, shown with an erect penis which he holds in his left hand and an upheld right arm holding a flail; by the New Kingdom he was fused with Amen in the deity Min-Amen-kamutef, Min-Amen-bull of his mother (Hathor), and his shrine was crowned with a pair of cow horns.

Mnevis - was the sacred bull of Heliopolis, later associated with Ra as the offspring of the solar cow deity, and possibly also with Min; when Akhenaten abandoned Amun (Amen) in favour of the Aten he claimed that he would maintain the Mnevis cult, which may have been because of its solar associations.

Mut (*also spelled Mout*) - mother, was originally a title of the primordial waters of the cosmos, the mother from which the cosmos emerged, as was Naunet in the Ogdoad cosmogony, however, the distinction between motherhood and cosmic water lead to the separation of these identities and Mut gained aspects of a creator goddess.

Naunet - a goddess, the primal waters from which all arose, similar to Mut and later closely related to Nu.

Neith - goddess of war, then great mother goddess - a name of the primal waters, the goddess of creation and weaving, said to weave all of the world on her loom.

Nekhbet - goddess depicted as an Egyptian vulture - protector of Egypt, royalty, and the pharaoh with her extended wings - referred to as Mother of Mothers, who hath existed from the Beginning, and Creatrix of the World (related to Wadjet); always seen on the front of pharaoh's double crown with Wadjet.

Nephthys (*also spelled Nebthet*) - goddess of death, holder of the rattle, the Sistrum - sister to Isis and the nursing mother of Horus and the pharaohs represented as the mistress of the temple, a woman with falcon wings, usually outstretched as a symbol of protection.

Nut - goddess of heaven and the sky - mother of many deities as well as the sun, the moon, and the stars.

Osiris (*also spelled Wesir*) - god of the underworld after Hathor and Anubis, fertility, and agriculture - the oldest son of the sky goddess, Nut, and the Earth god, Geb, and being brother and later, the husband of Isis - and early deity of Upper Egypt whose cult persisted into the sixth century BC.

Pakhet - she who tears, deity of merged aspects of Sekhmet and Bast, cult center at Beni Hasan where north and south met

- lioness protector, see Speos Artemidos.

Ptah - a creator deity, also god of craft.

Qebui - The "*Lord of the North Wind*," associated with the lands beyond the third cataract (i.e. Kush and the land of the Modern Sudan.

Ra - the sun, also a creator deity - whose chief cult centre was based in Heliopolis meaning "city of the sun".

Ra-Horakhty - god of both sky and Sun, a combination of Ra and Horus - thought to be god of the Rising Sun.

Reshep - war god who was originally from Syria.

Satis - the goddess who represented the flooding of the Nile River, ancient war, hunting, and fertility goddess, mother of the Nile, Anuket, associated with water, depicted with a bow and arrows, and a gazelle or antelope horned, and sometimes, feathered crown.

Sekhmet - goddess of destruction and war, the lioness - also personified as an aspect of Ra, fierce protector of the pharaoh, a solar deity, and later as an aspect of Hathor.

Seker (*also spelled Sokar*) - god of death.

Selket (*also spelled Serqet*) - scorpion goddess, protectress, goddess of magic.

Sobek - crocodile god of the Nile.

Set (*also spelled Seth*) - god of storms, later became god of evil, desert and patron of Upper Egypt - 'Set-animal'-headed- as one of the most promenant deities of chaos he does not have an actual animal to represent him, but is seen as an amalgamation of many different characteristics of other animals.

Seshat - goddess of writing, astronomy, astrology, architecture, and mathematics depicted as a scribe.

Shu - embodiment of wind or air.

Swenet - goddess of the ancient city on the border of southern Egypt at the Nile River, trade in hieroglyphs.

Tatenen (*also called Tenen or Tatjenen*) - Ancient Nature god. Later combined with Ptah as Ptah-tenen.

Taweret (*also spelled Tawret*) - goddess of pregnant women and protector at childbirth.

Tefnut - goddess, embodiment of rain, dew, clouds, and wet weather, depicted as a cat and sometimes as a lioness.

Thoth (*also spelled Djehuty*) - god of the moon, drawing, writing, geometry, wisdom, medicine, music, astronomy, magic; usually depicted as ibis-headed, or as a goose; cult centered in Khemennu

Wadjet - the goddess, snake goddess of lower Egypt, depicted as a cobra, patron and protector of Egypt and the pharaoh, always shown on crown of the pharaohs; later joined by the image of Nekhbet after north and south united; other symbols: eye, snake on staff.

Wadj-wer - fertility god and personification of the Mediterranean sea or lakes of the Nile delta.

Wepwawet - jackal god of upper Egypt.

Wosret - a localized guardian goddess, protector of the young god Horus, an early consort of Amun, who was later superseded by Mut.